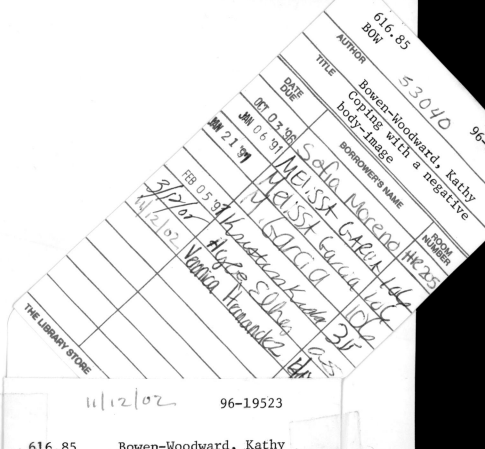

	616.85 BOW	53040	96-19523
AUTHOR			
TITLE	Bowen-Woodward, Kathy Coping with a negative body-image		
DATE DUE	BORROWER'S NAME		ROOM NUMBER
OCT 03 '96	Sofia Moreno		HR 205
JAN 06 '91	MELISSA GARCIA	lab	
JAN 21 '91	Melissa Garcia	lab	106
FEB 05 '97	M. Garcia		
3/7/01	Khristina Kuda		315
11/12/02	Hylee Esther		255
	Vanica Hernandez		

11/12/02   96-19523

616.85   Bowen-Woodward, Kathy
BOW   Coping with a negative
                         body-image

                 53040

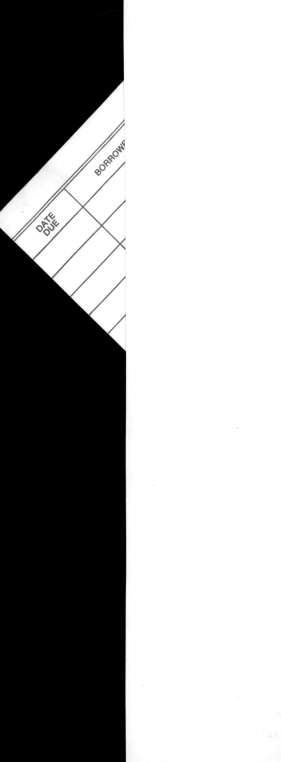

COPING WITH

A Negative Body-image

Kathy Bowen-Woodward, Ph.D.

THE ROSEN PUBLISHING GROUP, INC. / NEW YORK

Published in 1989 by The Rosen Publishing Group, Inc.
29 East 21st Street, New York, NY 10010

First Edition

Library of Congress Cataloging-In-Publication Data

Bowen-Woodward, Kathryn.
  Coping with a Negative Body-Image / Kathy Bowen-Woodward.
    p.   cm.
  Bibliography: p. 120
  Includes index.
  Summary: Advises the teen girl on viewing her body in a positive and healthy way so that diet and exercise programs don't get out of hand.
  1. Anorexia nervosa—Juvenile literature.   2. Bulimia—Juvenile literature.   3. Self-perception—Juvenile literature.
4. Teenagers—Health and hygiene—Juvenile literature.
[1. Self-perception.   2. Anorexia nervosa.   3. Bulimia.]
I. Title.
RC552.A5B69   1989   89-3583
616.85′2—dc19   CIP
                                                   AC

            53040

Manufactured in the U.S.A.

96-19523

ABOUT THE AUTHOR ◊

Kathy Bowen-Woodward has extensive experience treating patients with negative body-image, anorexia, and bulimia. She was Associate Clinical Director at The Renfrew Center, a residential facility for women with eating disorders, and remains a consultant there. She has given programs on eating disorders nationally and conducted workshops to train other professionals to work with patients with anorexia or bulimia.

At present she is Director of an Adult Partial Hospital Program, which treats a variety of patients including those with eating disorders. Although still interested in the treatment of anorexia and bulimia, she is currently writing and giving programs on the tendency of all American women to be dissatisfied with their bodies—not just those with eating disorders.

Dr. Bowen-Woodward holds a B.A. from the University of Colorado, and an M.A. in Community Psychology and a Ph.D. in Clinical Psychology from Temple University. She lives with her husband and teenage daughter in Virginia Beach, Virginia.

To my daughter,
Hilary,
with the hope
that she will grow
into a woman
who is comfortable
with herself
and her body.

Contents

Introduction—
How It Can Happen

It didn't end up the way she'd planned—all she had wanted to do was look better and be more fit. She'd been looking at herself in the full-length mirror, getting ready for a school dance, and nothing had looked right. After the fourth outfit, she had begun to think that maybe the problem wasn't the clothes—maybe it was herself. As she turned around and looked at herself carefully, she noticed bulges she had never really seen before and realized that she was getting fat. She knew that the past few years had brought changes to her body, and frankly she hadn't liked some of them, but now as she looked with a critical eye she saw that things had gotten out of hand. Her waist was too big and her arms looked too heavy and her thighs touched as she stood there, and, well, there wasn't anything about her that looked right.

She was appalled and disgusted and wondered how she could have let herself get this way. No wonder boys didn't ask her out and she wasn't friends with the popular girls. She had to do something about her body and do it seriously. She decided to go on a strict diet to lose five or ten pounds and begin a vigorous exercise program to tighten and tone her body and make it presentable. She felt a sense of hope and excitement as she began to visualize what her new life would be like when she was thin and fit, and she felt a rush of pleasure at the thought of taking control of things.

In the beginning it was actually fun. She planned breakfasts of grapefruit, lunches of salad, and dinners of lean meat and vegetables. And there would be no snacking between meals! She started an exercise program that left her sore in the beginning, but somehow the pain felt good because it reminded her that she was doing something—she was making a better body. She got up every morning in time to run before school (she, who used to have trouble getting up at even a normal time!), and she exercised with an aerobic video when she came home before starting her homework. Gradually, she began to feel better about herself, particularly since the scale each morning showed that she was winning. She was losing weight and feeling firmer, and people were noticing. Friends made comments such as "Gosh, you're looking great these days," or "I don't know what you're doing, but it's sure working." Even the clothes that she had tried on for the dance that night were loose on her now. Life was good, and she felt better about herself than she had in a long time.

Gradually she lost five pounds and then ten, but somehow it didn't feel like enough. In fact, it felt like only the beginning. She looked at herself carefully in the mirror every day now and saw what she had accomplished, but she also saw how much more she had to do. She wondered how she had ever tolerated all that flab she had carried, and she planned how her exercise and careful diet would carve away even more inches.

She never really noticed when it stopped being fun and began to feel like pressure. The light diet that had initially been so exciting no longer was satisfying. She longed for some junk food but was afraid that if she ate even one french fry she would blow up to her old weight again. She was exercising more now than in the beginning, but it still didn't feel like enough. In fact, she was fifteen pounds lighter than she had been when she started, but she still felt fat. Some days when she got on the scale she found she had actually gained a pound from the day before. On those days she could never quite shake the feeling of disgust that settled on her. The kids at school had stopped telling her how terrific she looked, and some even said she was getting too thin. Increasingly, she felt that she was on a treadmill that wasn't going forward anymore but was taking all she had to keep from going backward. She felt desperate and unhappy, and she decided that the only things she could rely on were her exercise and diet. In fact, on days when she missed any part of her workout she felt instantly fat and unattractive. At least when she put in a good run or workout she felt good about herself—if only for the moment.

The above story represents a composite of histories from people I have known and treated over the years. At this point the story could go in a number of directions.

- She could develop the condition of anorexia nervosa, in which she would focus all her energy on drastically reducing her calorie intake and increasing the amount of exercise. Her sense of well-being would rest solely on her success in these two areas. She might pursue this course even to the point of serious illness or death.

- She might discover that she could not tolerate the food deprivation and could develop bulimia, in which she would permit herself to consume huge quantities of food and then purge it either through vomiting, laxatives, excessive exercise, or a combination of the three. She would spend more and more of her time and energy on consuming and then purging food, leaving little time for anything else.
- She might continue—as many girls and women in this country do—to focus on her body as the solution to life's problems, never feeling really satisfied with herself and looking to diet or exercise or both for accomplishment and success.
- She might move back and forth between these scenarios.

No matter how the story proceeds, she has a body-image problem. That means that she is preoccupied with how she looks and has lost the ability to see herself and know how she appears to the world. Unfortunately, this misperception of her body is a negative one; she tends to see herself as ugly or fat or having thighs that are too big or a stomach that isn't flat enough or breasts that are too full—even if others see her much more positively. She has made her body the enemy and is using most of her energy to fight it. That's a very difficult relationship to have with your own body—even in the easiest of times, and we all know that adolescence is not the easiest of times. It is a time of change and development, and what the person in our story has done is to stop development. She didn't start out to do that. She started out to try to feel better about herself and looked at her body and thought, "There's the culprit!" But what she had done is stop a lot of things—such as the chance to find other sources for good feelings about herself, or the chance to discover that her body is just one of a number of ways to tell the world who she is, or the chance to develop other aspects of herself as she grows up.

This book is about negative body-image—what it is, where it comes from, ways to think about it, and possibilities for making it better. This is not a diet book. It will not make you thinner or trimmer or bigger in some places and stronger in others. But it may give you ways to think that will help you make the decisions that are best for you about your body's shape.

This book is written primarily for and about girls. That does not mean that, if you're a boy, you can't use it, or that there's anything wrong with you if you recognize yourself in places where I am talking about girls. Males are beginning to catch up with females in needing to have their bodies be trimmer and look a certain way in order to feel acceptable. But for the most part it is girls who struggle (and have struggled historically) to make their bodies do the things their culture demands. It is much more common for girls to consider their body the most important factor in whether they can feel good about themselves. And it is girls and women who account for about 90 percent of those who become involved with the disorders of body-image: anorexia and bulimia. So, with the exception of Chapter 6, I shall generally talk about females, but what I say could apply to you even if you are a boy.

The format of the book is a chapter to discuss a topic followed by exercises that help you think about yourself in relation to that topic. The text should give you some new information, but the real work takes place when you sit quietly and explore.

If an exercise calls for thinking, try to do it when you won't be interrupted. You may be tempted to try to do all the exercises at once. Don't. To be most useful, each one should be given time to be fully explored and then rested—much like dough after you've kneaded it. Sometimes the most important thing you'll discover doesn't happen during the exercise but later when you're not even looking for it.

CHAPTER 1

Making Your Body the Problem

LEARNING WHAT'S WHAT

Our body-image is just one of the ways we think about ourselves. But before we look at this specific way, let's consider how people decide what they're supposed to be and how they're supposed to look in the first place.

One of the ways we decide what we should be is to look around and see what other people are doing and how they look while they're doing it. We look at our family and friends and strangers we pass and people we admire. We look at people on television and in movies and magazines. We are always gathering information about how we should be. When we are very young we look to our immediate family, but as we grow older we tend to look to a broader group for information about what's okay and what isn't. In the beginning we look around to learn how to do the things we see everyone else doing—like walking and talking. As we grow older, we often look to see how we measure up or to check on how we're doing. No one wants to feel foolish or do things wrong, so we work hard to be what we think we're supposed to be. We do this all our lives and often without questioning or even thinking about it. We human beings are remarkable in our ability to absorb information unthinkingly and let it influence how we see ourselves.

So what happens if, as you're looking around, you get information saying that something about you isn't OK? Well, if it's learning that you're not supposed to yell in the library, that's useful to discover and will probably save you from future criticism. But what if you look at TV and magazines and come to believe that your body is ugly because it isn't as slender as the ones you see. That could be trouble.

Let's imagine that you are a healthy teenage girl who happens to have a nice roundish body. You're not obese; there's no health risk involved—you just don't look like the women that advertising pays to sell its products. Now, what if you decide that because you don't look like the models something is wrong with you? Then it gets unhealthy. Now you believe that something is wrong with who you are just because your body doesn't conform to the shape that is currently considered marketable. That is an unhealthy way to think because you may stop accepting who you are and begin to dislike whatever parts you think are wrong. Worse yet, you may try to remake yourself in the image of the magazines. So what's wrong with that? Nothing, if you do it reasonably and with moderation and keep your perspective on its importance. But many of you don't do it that way. Let me tell you a story.

*   *   *

Once upon a time there was a gardener who loved small trees. He didn't like trees that were tall and full—only small and dainty ones, and he planted all varieties of them in his grove. One year he noticed a young tree coming up that he hadn't planted. Normally, he grew only trees that he had carefully selected, but this tree had leaves that were a nice almond shape and a trunk with nice texture and lovely coloring, so he decided to let it stay. The tree grew, and the gardener became unhappy because it wasn't small like the others but had a large trunk and full branches. So he decided that he would make this tree small like the others. First he chopped off its long and bushy branches and cut its trunk to a shorter height. Then he stopped giving it water regularly as he did the other trees and built a shade around it so that it wouldn't get so much sun. He believed that if he held back nourishment the tree would stop growing and become small and dainty like the other trees in his grove. Gradually the tree did stop growing, but instead of becoming a small dainty tree, it became a large tree that never grew. Its trunk was full and ready to support many branches, but they had all been cut away. The sparse new growth it had managed to generate without proper sun and water was spindly and unhealthy. One day when the gardener stopped by, he saw that the bark had lost its lovely coloring and the leaves had become thin and curled. The trunk that had been large and tall now looked silly at the shorter height. The gardener shook his head sadly and said, "What have I done? Instead of creating the tree I wanted, I have ruined the tree I had."

*   *   *

All over this country girls are trying to do with themselves what the gardener tried to do to his tree. They have looked around and decided that something is wrong with the way they are built, and they are trying to change themselves. They may hate one part of their body or be generally dissatisfied with the whole thing, but they are trying to remake what they have into something they don't have. They believe that somehow they can do it if only they try hard enough, use enough self-discipline, or show enough restraint. They spend enormous amounts of energy on this; and they feel good about themselves if they think they are succeeding and bad about themselves if they think they are failing. But like the gardener, they can never really succeed as they think they can. And they hurt the body they have while trying to create the body they want.

AMANDA

Amanda was fourteen and the youngest of three daughters. She lived with her parents in a small town in the Northeast. Her mother was a secretary for a local business, and her father was a plumber. Her older sisters had done well in high school and now were in college and doing well there too. They were the first members of her family ever to go to college, and her parents were very proud. Amanda had trouble with school. She had to work very hard to make the kind of grades that her parents seemed to expect and that her teachers who had taught her sisters expected as well. It made her feel stupid, as if it were somehow her fault that she wasn't smarter, as if somehow she weren't something she was supposed to be.

Amanda was not like her sisters in another important way: They tended to look like their father's side of the family—tall and slender. She looked more like her mother's side—shorter and rounded. She was 5'3", had full hips and thighs, and was a bit chunky. Amanda had always envied her sisters and wished she could look like them. She felt ugly and unattractive and angry at herself that she looked that way. It didn't seem fair that she was "fat" and her sisters were "thin." It made her feel as though somehow, once again, she wasn't something she was supposed to be.

It was during her junior year that she decided to do something about it. She decided to go on a diet to lose weight. She knew exactly how she wanted to look. She was going to look even better than her sisters. She wanted to look like a model she had seen in *Seventeen* magazine, tall with long slender legs, almost no hips, a very small bottom, a tiny waist, and small breasts.

Amanda knew she could do this if she just stuck to her diet and put her heart into it. She taped the picture of the model on her bedroom wall and a picture of a pig on the refrigerator—to remind her of what she could look like if she stayed on the diet and what she would continue to look like if she didn't.

Right from the beginning, she lost weight. Her mother was supportive because she knew her daughter was a little "heavy" (she had always felt that way herself) and was pleased to see her doing something about it. Her father said he was glad that she was taking an interest in her appearance. Gradually, she weighed less and less just as she wanted to. She was excited and pleased that her plan was working, that she would soon look just like the model.

Only she didn't. No matter how much weight she lost, she didn't look right. She decided it was because she wasn't thin enough, so she just kept on dieting and losing more and more weight. In time, she lost weight all over her body. She lost her stomach, her waist became thin, her breasts shrank, and her thighs and hips disappeared. But some things happened that she hadn't expected. Her face and neck became thin and hollow-looking, her rib cage began to show, her arms and legs became skinny and had poor muscle tone, her hair began to thin and fall out, and she stopped having her periods. She had lost so much weight that she looked sickly and emaciated. Even though she had tried her hardest, she hadn't been able to make her body fit her idea of how a body should look. It didn't seem fair, and Amanda thought that maybe she still needed to lose more weight.

BUILDING A SELF-IMAGE

What does this have to do with negative body-image? A lot. Each of us develops a self-image, which is basically the image or notion of ourselves that we walk around with each day. This self-image is the sum total of all the ways we evaluate ourselves in all the things we do. It stems from our experience of ourselves in a large number of places and a variety of roles. You might think of it as a bank where you have a large number of accounts. In this bank called "How I Feel About Myself" are accounts that might include: "as a daughter," "as a student," "in a bathing suit," "as an athlete," "as a girlfriend," "as a sister," and so on. We can think about ourselves in an almost endless number of ways to develop a sense of who we are. Generally we find that some accounts contain more than others. That's important to remember when we go to the bank. For example, someone who has very little athletic ability would not want to keep drawing on the "as an athlete" account for good feelings about herself.

Well, that's the way it's supposed to work. But it doesn't seem to be working that way anymore. Many of us have only one account in the bank: "Am I thin enough?" This means that even if we do well in school, are a cheerleader, have good friends, or are a good dancer, none of that is enough to let us feel good about ourselves. It's treated as stuff that's expected but not really valued. That's a crazy way to run a bank, and if we were on Wall Street we'd be out of business.

But there's something that makes this banking system even crazier. When we look at the models in the magazines or the women on TV to see whether we are thin enough, we forget that these models are "abnormally" built. Their figures do not generally occur in nature. They work very hard to develop their bodies, and they have to work constantly to maintain what they have created. For every model we see in a magazine, there are many who were turned away because they were too tall or too heavy or just didn't have the right "look." This means that when we look at a model, we're looking at the rare exception rather than the general rule. We're seeing what you can be *if* you have just the right ingredients to begin with, *if* you work unceasingly to bring your body within certain limits, *if* you are continually preoccupied with your body, *if* you have a team of professionals doing your wardrobe, and *if* you are very lucky. Yet most of us don't think about that when we look at the newspapers or magazines. We think we're looking to see how we're supposed to look. We think we're just making sure we're OK.

And we decide we're not. So we start to diet and exercise and skip meals and do all the things we think will let us look like the models, and if only we can look like them we'll be OK. But since few of us can look like them, most of us end up on a cycle that goes nowhere but leaves us chronically dissatisfied and preoccupied with our bodies. And that's one of the ways negative body-image begins.

CHARLOTTE

Charlotte was fifteen and an only child. She lived with her parents in a large city in Georgia in an expensive suburban home. Her father was a plastic surgeon and very well known and respected. Her mother spent a lot of time on charitable causes and was active in the Junior League. Charlotte thought they loved each other, but sometimes she wasn't sure. The didn't yell at each other or anything like that. They just didn't seem very friendly sometimes.

Her mother had been on a diet as long as Charlotte could remember. She was always worrying about her weight and going to the club to work out. She played tennis three times a week when weather permitted and was always tan and attractive. People always said to Charlotte, "My, you have such a lovely mother." Charlotte thought she was pretty too—prettier than her daughter.

Charlotte did well in school and was fairly popular. But she worried a lot about how she looked and spent a long time each morning choosing her outfit and putting on her makeup. She thought she had an OK figure—she wasn't really fat or anything—but she didn't look as good as some of the other girls at school, and she sure didn't look like the girls in the magazines. She didn't even look as good as her mother. She thought she needed to lose a few pounds. It was mainly her thighs; she thought they were too big. And her stomach needed to be a bit flatter and tighter. Sometimes her father walked by and said, "Hold in that stomach!" She hated it when he did that, and she hated herself for not holding it in.

Charlotte started a serious diet in her freshman year. She lost a few pounds and felt a little better. As the year went on, however, she found those pounds creeping back on. So she went on another diet and lost them again, but they came back. It seemed as though she would have to be just like her mother—always on a diet. Well, if that's what it was going to take, she'd do it. After all, everyone appreciated what it did for her mother. Perhaps dieting was just part of becoming a woman.

Exercises

Make a list of the people you admire. Write down what you admire about them. Is it their looks? Their attitudes? Their accomplishments? Is there anyone on your list who might be considered a little heavy? Who on your list influences you most about how you should look? Is this realistic?

Imagine your own Bank of Self-esteem. What accounts are full? What accounts are empty? What account do you draw on most often when you want to feel good about yourself? Given what is in that account, is that realistic? What accounts never have any activity? Would it help you to rethink how you use your accounts and change the way you do your banking?

Imagine you are a tree in a grove. What kind of tree are you? Are you tall and full? Or small and spindly? Or short and bushy? It you were to let yourself grow naturally, with full sun and water, how would you look? Do you ever treat yourself the way the gardener treated his tree? Do you want to keep on doing that?

Here is a checklist for signs of negative body-image. If you recognize yourself in the following, your body-image is at risk.

1. Do you find yourself always worrying about what you eat and getting angry or disgusted with yourself because you ate too much?
2. Do you weigh yourself at least once a day and feel ugly or fat if you weigh more than a certain number?
3. Can your day be ruined if you weigh too much or eat too much?
4. Do you find that you can feel OK about your weight one minute and feel fat the next, particularly if something upsetting happens?
5. Do you sometimes stay home from a party or get-together if you feel fat?
6. Do you feel heavy even though most people consider your weight fine?
7. Do you look at magazines and think models are "normal" weight?
8. Do you constantly check your stomach and feel

disgusted with yourself if it feels fat and pleased
with yourself if it feels flat?

9. If you miss your exercise for one day are you
miserable and do you feel fat? Even if you felt a
comfortable weight the day before?

10. Do you think your weight is the most important
factor in your happiness?

CHAPTER 2

Let's Take a Look

at Bodies

A HISTORICAL PERSPECTIVE

Many of you who are worried that you're too big here or too big there may not realize that what is considered too big or too small has changed throughout the years. While there is an ideal of female thinness in America today, it hasn't always been so. In fact, observers of cultural trends suggest that what has been considered the ideal female body has moved like a pendulum back and forth from full-figured and voluptuous to thin and angular.

In the late 1800s the ideal American woman was full-figured and buxom. Hips were emphasized, and the ideal woman had measurements something like 36–26–38. She kept her figure in place with a corset, a tight-fitting undergarment that rigidly controlled her shape from her breasts to her hips. By 1900 a new image had evolved. The "Gibson Girl" with her sway back and hourglass figure was the look women wanted. She was slenderer than her predecessor but still had accentuated hips and breasts and her corset pulled tight.

The 1920s brought the "flapper" who bobbed her hair, got rid of the corset, and wore short, loose-fitting dresses. She was flat-chested (or bound her breasts to make them flat) and was supposed to have no hips. I'm not sure what the woman with a figure was supposed to do with it—unless it was just wait until the the tide turned again. Which it did in the 1950's. This decade marked the return of the full-figured, voluptuous female body, with movie stars like Jayne Mansfield and Marilyn Monroe typifying the feminine ideal. The popular "sweater girl" look was in, with a cinched-in waist to emphasize the return to full breasts. Women not so well endowed were left feeling inferior, and many resorted to using "falsies"—pads that fit into the bra cup.

The 1960s promoted the flat-chested and hipless look again, this time with a British teenager named Twiggy as its champion. At 5'7" and 92 pounds, Twiggy looked out at us from magazine covers with large mascaraed eyes and a young boy's body and made any of us with round-ness feel all wrong. Now a woman who wanted to feel beautiful and feminine needed to lose any sign that she was female. This era, not surprisingly, brought with it a surge of anorexia among teenage girls. I suppose that since the magazines were saying women should look as if they were starving, adolescent girls took the culture at its word. Beginning with the mid-1970s, the feminine ideal began to allow a bit more breast and hip than the Twiggy look, but it has never returned to the volup-tuous figure of the 1950s. The current feminine image demands a body that is carefully sculpted through vigorous exercise, careful eating, and a lot of attention.

Although nearly every culture has tried to impose a shape on the female body, not all have valued thinness the way the current culture does. In fact, most cultures have preferred a plump female figure with full breasts and rounded hips (and that includes ample thighs!). But there is something about large size in a woman's body that we consider unfeminine and something about narrow hips and small upturned breasts that seems so attractive. Think about it a minute, though. Narrow hips are what most of us have *before* we develop and mature as women, and small breasts are what many of us have *on the way* to developing larger ones. And big is what many of us would become if we *didn't* start worrying about what we eat as soon as we start to grow up. The theme here seems to be to keep women young and undeveloped. It's worth thinking about.

The concept of the corset is also worth a few thoughts. For hundreds of years it compressed women's figures, made it almost impossible for them to bend over or breathe, and hurt to wear. But it was considered a necessary sacrifice for any woman who wanted to look attractive. Sometimes it was used to make hips smaller, sometimes to make them larger. Sometimes it pushed waists and breasts up, and sometimes it pushed them down. But it was always there to make women's bodies something they weren't, and it was symbolic of how their bodies were not naturally sound and attractive but needed support and direction. The corset was responsible for withered muscles, broken ribs, and atrophied organs, but women wore it—even successful and powerful women. Queen Elizabeth I was one of its earliest advocates and used its eighty pounds of pressure to fashion her famous wasp waist.

The corset went out of style during World War I. What seems disturbing, however, is that even though the corset is a thing of the past (and we sometimes laugh that women actually wore such a thing) we *still* wear one. Only now we don't put the corset on from the outside; we create it from the inside. All of us who want our body to be this or that particular shape no longer do it with steel and elastic. We go one step further—we change who we actually are. We remake ourselves in the image that is currently popular (and, I suppose, will remake ourselves again when that image changes).

DIFFERENT BODY TYPES

OK. We've looked at how powerfully the culture can influence us to believe that something is attractive and how capriciously that something can change. Let's look at the various ways bodies come in the first place. A man named W. H. Sheldon developed a classification of body types according to such criteria as muscularity, bone development, and degree of softness and roundness. He described three main body types found throughout the world: ectomorphic, mesomorphic, and endomorphic. The ectomorph tends to be slender and angular in build; the mesomorph is generally stocky and muscular; and the endomorph is heavyset and rounded. According to Sheldon, few of us are a pure body type, but many of us tend to be more like one type than another. If you happen to fit into one of these body types fairly easily, it might be a useful classification for you to use to learn about your body's shape and its limitations. It's important to know your body's natural tendencies and what is realistically possible for you.

I'm not convinced, however, that these body types are as useful for females as they are for males. Female bodies tend to have areas such as hips and breasts that are not adequately covered by Sheldon's classifications, and these are among the areas that most girls worry about.

So how might we try to think about female bodies? Well, existing attempts include such descriptions as "pear-shaped," which suggests that the bottom is larger than the top; or "hourglass," which signifies a wasplike waist between fuller breasts and hips; or "full-figured," which suggests that everything is bigger than the models'.

I think what is needed, but has not been developed, is a way of thinking about the female body that is nonjudgmental, descriptive, and includes the various dimensions that make up the body in female form. Perhaps we could simply put various categories on a continuum and note where each of us falls: softer—harder, rounder—straighter, taller—shorter, wider—thinner, bigger—smaller, more breast—less breast, more hip—less hip, and so on. In that way we would not be limited by anything other than the number of adjectives we can think of to put on a continuum. If someone wanted to think about her body type she could note whether she was more or less or these things and whether the model she wanted to look like seemed to be more or less of the same things. This is really important, because if you set out to look a certain way you need to know whether it's even possible.

Let's say you see a picture of a model whom you want to resemble. She is taller, thinner, straighter, and less hip and breast, and you are shorter, rounder, and more breast and hip. You could diet your whole life and exercise ten hours a day seven days a week and you would never look like that model. You have different ingredients—will bake into a different kind of cake. You have a different design—will be a different kind of car. You have a different body and will become a different shape. No matter how you think about it, your capacity to be anything you want physically is influenced and limited by your body type. We don't seem to have trouble with this concept anywhere but with our bodies. We don't expect a Chevrolet to become a Porsche. We don't expect jonquil bulbs to grow into roses. But we expect our bodies to be what we want, whatever the culture says is currently appreciated.

Maybe part of the problem is that our culture needs to appreciate a greater variety of shapes so that developing girls can appreciate themselves regardless of their physical packaging. There's something dehumanizing about a society that says to its emerging women, "Welcome... but only if you look a certain way." No wonder those of us who don't fit the mold frantically work to remake ourselves. But perhaps what needs to be remade is not us, but the cultural attitudes.

FAMILY INFLUENCES

Another way to think about your body's natural limited capacity is to look at your family. What kind of body does your mother have? Your father? Sisters and brothers? What do your grandparents look like? Are these people small-framed and tiny? Do they have full hips? Do they tend to be heavy? Are they tall and high-waisted or of average height and long-waisted? Do they diet all the time to be what they are? Can they eat a lot and still be skinny? Sometimes one side of the family looks one way and the other side looks another. Does everyone look the same, or are there big differences within your family? Whom do you resemble most in your body shape? These are important questions because they address your body's natural predisposition. That means what your body is most likely to become. If you're going to spend a lot of energy trying to look a certain way, I'd sure feel better if you knew, going into it, whether you even had a chance of succeeding.

LORETTA

Loretta was fifteen and lived with her parents, her grandparents, and her fraternal twin Francis in a large rowhouse in the Northeast. Her house was frequently visited by relatives who lived nearby, and there was always the smell of something good cooking in the kitchen. Her mother believed in "family"; she always had somebody over for something and fed them while they were there.

Loretta and her brother didn't look much like twins. When they had been younger they had resembled one another, and people had called them "two peas in a pod." But as they'd gotten older differences had begun to emerge. Now Francis was taller and slenderer like his grandfather on his father's side, and Loretta was shorter and heavier like her mother and grandmother. These days when people learned they were twins they laughed and exclaimed, "You don't look it!" And it was true. Except for their coloring, they didn't look like two peas anymore—they looked more like a carrot and a pear.

Loretta hated her hips and thighs. She felt miserable when she saw herself in the mirror, and she tried to imagine how she would look if she could strip away the horrible fat. Her mother told her she was silly and that men liked women with some meat on their bones, but Loretta didn't believe her. She hated being a member of this family where all the women were chubby and only a few lucky men were slender. She sometimes hated Francis because he had gotten the good body, and she felt it was unfair that she hadn't.

It was funny that nobody seemed to dislike her because of her looks, but she believed her life would be happier if she could only look different. She knew that her aunts and uncles and cousins loved her, and her girlfriends liked her too. But most of them looked the way she did. When they got together for a slumber party or pizza on a Saturday night, they would plan how they would go on a diet and wake up thin and trim. In fact, it was their joke with one another. When they were sitting around going through magazines and looking at the beautiful models, they would say, "Maybe we'll wake up tomorrow morning and be thin and trim!" And everybody would laugh and have another piece of pizza.

But Loretta couldn't laugh about it anymore. She had grown to hate herself because of her looks. She decided to go on a diet and try to lose the extra poundage on her hips and thighs. That was all. She knew she couldn't be tall like Francis, but she could at least be slender.

Her mother thought it was a phase that she would get over and humored her. She was allowed to skip the heavy dinners and make herself something light. Her father thought it was all foolishness, but he had a stomach that hung over his belt and Loretta thought he was hardly in a position to comment.

Loretta worked on her diet for a full six months. She ate less and less and lost weight but not in the right places. She couldn't believe it. She was doing all she could—sometimes she even felt faint from hunger—and still she had heavier thighs and hips than she thought acceptable. What more could she do? How could she be attractive if dieting wouldn't work? She couldn't believe that she might have to live out her life with the body she'd been born with. She couldn't believe there wasn't something she could do to reshape it.

Exercises

Make a list of your relatives and sketch their general body shapes beside their names. What kinds of bodies do you see? What kinds don't you see? What seems to be your family's tendency in bodies? What about these findings pleases you? What scares you? What would be realistic for you to expect your body to look like?

Stand in front of a full-length mirror, undressed, and look at your body. Try not to be critical (you'll be surprised how hard it is not to be); just be curious. Imagine your body as a landscape, not as something that isn't what you want it to be. Where does your body get smallest? Where is it largest? What shape are your legs? Your arms? What does your torso look like? Do you have a small waist or does your body line tend to be straight? Is your body egg-shaped or more like a pear? Or an hourglass? What things do you notice that I haven't mentioned? Few of us ever really see ourselves as we are; see how honestly you can look at your body. Is there any part of your body that you can appreciate? If so, do it now. Is there a part of your body you would like to change? How realistic is that wish?

Does your body fit the ideal of another era better than the one you're in? Does it seem fair to punish yourself for this misfit? What does it do to your sense of self-appreciation to find fault with your body? Is this what you want for yourself?

CHAPTER 3

Reeducating Yourself about Female Form

CHANGES AND MORE CHANGES

So many of you have such specific notions of what you're supposed to look like. I wonder how many of you know how nature has designed you to look. Since it's during normal adolescent development that most girls start fighting the ways their bodies start growing, it seems important to understand the natural physical changes that occur during this period.

Men and women are built differently. No news there. Until puberty they grow in a fairly similar pattern and show no striking differences in height or weight or muscle strength. That all changes with the onset of puberty—that time, beginning about ten or eleven for girls, when they have a height spurt, begin to menstruate, and develop secondary sexual characteristics.

The first difference between the sexes is that most girls begin puberty about two years ahead of most boys.

That means that girls start changing way ahead of boys, and sometimes that feels uncomfortable—especially if you're one of the first girls on your block to grow taller or develop breasts.

A second difference has to do with the distribution of subcutaneous fat—fat that is deposited under the skin. Humans accumulate subcutaneous fat several times during their lives. Among these are the first year of life (which is why babies are so plump), during prepubescence (which is why many seven- or eight-year-olds look "chubby"), and during adolescence for females. The sites of these female adolescent deposits are the breasts, thighs, abdomen, buttocks, upper back, and backs of upper arms. Males don't have a similar pattern of fat deposits but tend to become more muscular as they move through adolescence, developing broader shoulders and a thinner waist. But girls develop a rounder figure as a natural result of their body's transformation during puberty. And that is what is so hard for many girls.

The difficulty seems to stem from a couple of factors. First, as I mentioned, the transformation generally occurs before boys start to change, and it is often drastic and swift. Not for all—some girls worry that their bodies will *never* change. But many girls feel that almost overnight their body has gone from one they felt familiar with to a stranger's body that they now inhabit. It goes from one that felt safe and comfortable to one that often feels uncomfortable and sometimes unsafe. It is easy for a girl to feel literally out of control by her body's rapid changing and depressed by her powerlessness to stop the process.

Another potential difficulty for girls is that as they

develop a few new bulges "in the right places," their relationship with the world—and perhaps themselves— is irrevocably changed. As their body begins to show their new physical development, others (particularly male others) begin to act differently toward them. Girls quickly discover that their body is now a sexual one with powers they can't always control.

A girl may notice that her father begins to act more distant and less comfortable with her now that she has developed this new body. Or boys who have heretofore been good friends may start to behave differently. In the world at large, she may begin to get attention and recognition that wasn't there before. Maybe all this attention feels OK, and then again maybe it doesn't. Maybe boys start saying suggestive things, or maybe she just notices that they're treating or looking at her differently. But the feeling many girls get, as they develop and mature physically, is that males begin to behave as though they want something and it has something to do with this new body. Sometimes it's a distant message, like whistles or wolf-calls as she walks by, and sometimes it's much closer, like when she's out with a boy and things start to get physical. But it's new, and it often feels like a demand. And all this just because her body has changed. That can be pretty hard for a girl to deal with and understand sometimes. Like what's important here—me or my body? It's a fair question and one that girls who have grown into women continue to ask.

HOW YOU SEE THE PACKAGE

Another problem for girls and their developing bodies is the difference in how they think about their bodies compared to the way males do. Although men are becoming more like females in this regard, as fashion and the media make them more body-conscious, the difference usually still holds. Typically, if you ask a male about his body he will say, "It's OK," or "It could be bigger," or "I wish I could lose a little weight." But that's it. He tends to see his body as a single unit that's OK or needs a little work. If you ask a female the same question, she will typically break her body down into many different parts about which she has strong feelings one way or the other. For instance, she may tell you that her thighs are too big, her waist is too fat, her breasts are too small, her upper arms are too flabby, her calves are too small, her upper back has too much weight, her ankles are too fat, and so on.

This tendency to break the body into discrete parts and focus on each one separately is dangerous. It means that even if you're satisfied with the way you look in a couple of areas, you're bound to be dissatisfied with a couple of places. And that means you focus on those negative parts and feel bad about yourself because of them. It's a kind of crazy, perfectionistic thinking that does us no good and gets us into a lot of trouble. It leaves us chronically dissatisfied with our physical packaging and unable to get on to other things. It leaves us stuck forever trying to fix our bodies and never really getting on to the important work of growing up and maturing.

BACKWARD WHILE YOU GO FORWARD

Another source of a girl's discomfort stems from another difference between the sexes. As boys progress through adolescence, they tend to move toward the male cultural ideal. They generally become bigger and stronger and more muscular. But for girls the progress through adolescence takes them away from the cultural ideal, which tends to embrace the prepubescent body with just a few carefully selected curves. Thus a teenage girl who is getting roundness and softness and hips just as Mother Nature intended is becoming less attractive according to cultural guidelines. The response of most teenage girls is to be horrified by what adolescence brings and do their best to stamp it out. They look at their body's "natural" development as something "unnatural" and wrong, and they feel fat and unattractive. And the easy remedy for that problem is to go on a diet to get rid of, or at least slow down or minimize, the new developments.

In essence, girls don't want to be girls; they want to be something else—not quite boys but, in terms of percent of body fat and shape, not quite girls. That's a ticklish position because it commits them to not being what they are. And it will require steady, constant, and unremitting work to keep away what wants to be there. I suppose it's a choice that a girl can make, but at least she ought to know what she's up against. She's fighting her very biology, and it's a fight that will require an enormous amount of energy even to reach a stand-off. That energy won't be available to meet other challenges that she'll encounter or to develop abilities that would bolster her self-esteem more reliably than the elusive perfect body. Seems like a set-up: Keep females preoccupied with their bodies and they'll never get to the really important issues. Somehow you've got to wonder about a culture that lets a girl feel fat simply because her body has taken its natural female form and that encourages her to fight against herself rather than enjoy self-acceptance.

MARILYN

Marilyn was nineteen and a sophomore in college. She had grown up in the South, living mainly in Florida and South Carolina, and had an older sister who was married and a younger brother who still lived at home. Marilyn had been an "early maturer." She had begun menstruating when she was ten years old and developed breasts about the same time. She had been painfully self-conscious about both, but particularly her breasts. Not only had she developed early but she had developed large. She couldn't hide them, and some of her friends had teased her mercilessly. She suspected some of the girls had been jealous and their teasing had been a bit mean. But the boys had been kind of funny about it, as if they were interested in her because of these things she had grown. Some of the younger boys called them her "personality" and wanted to touch them. Some of the older boys had wanted her to go out with them. Marilyn's response to all of this had been to withdraw and become very shy. She felt painfully uncomfortable about her body and tried to wear clothes that deemphasized her deformity (as she had come to regard it). She never wore anything tight or form-fitting and stuck to clothes that were baggy and loose. For the first couple of years, before other girls caught up with her, she refused to wear a bathing suit in the summer; she simply never went swimming.

By the time she was thirteen Marilyn had become

somewhat anorectic. She dieted heavily, lost a lot of weight (including in her breasts), and felt much more comfortable with herself. Her family were a little worried about the weight loss, but her older sister was very slender and her parents decided that perhaps Marilyn had needed slimming down.

Throughout high school, Marilyn worked hard to keep her weight down and watched her diet very carefully. She exercised religiously every day and never let herself enjoy junk food. She felt comfortable with herself when she was thin and panicked whenever her weight went up even a pound. She had managed to achieve a body she could live with and was was afraid to let it get out of control as it had when she had begun puberty.

Her first year of college was hard for her. She had more trouble academically than she had experienced before and found it hard to make friends. Her roommate was sloppy and kept their room a mess. Marilyn had always kept her room at home very neat, and she felt depressed and unhappy with all the disarray. She and her roommate didn't fight about it because Marilyn didn't say anything. She didn't want to make a big fuss, so she just felt upset inside.

She also found it hard to be as restrictive with her food. At home, her mother had agreed not to bring fattening foods into the house, but at school they were everywhere. Every social function had a table with mountains of cookies and chips and dip, and the cafeteria served mainly fried foods and other high-calorie fare. Gradually, she found herself eating more—foods she'd wanted for years and never let herself have. It felt a little uneasy to be doing something that felt wrong, but it sure tasted good.

Until she began to gain weight. Then she had a re-awakening of all those horrible feelings she had had when she was ten and eleven. She was terrified but didn't think she could stop eating. So she started eating and throwing up. Not a bad solution. Until it started to take more and more of her time and she began to feel more and more depressed. But there was no way out of it. She couldn't gain weight. Those feelings of her body being out of control were just too painful.

Exercises

Think back to when you started to feel "fat." Was it about the time that you began to develop? What were your feelings about your body and yourself at that time? Were you comfortable with your body's changes? Were you uncomfortable? What did you wish your body would do? What did you wish it wouldn't do? What did you try to make it do?

Think about your body now. What areas do you feel most uncomfortable with? Do they correspond to the areas where females naturally have fat deposits? Does that change how you feel about them? Why?

How do you feel about the female form? How do you feel about the male form? Which one are you more comfortable with for yourself? Why?

How do you generally feel about your body? Do you break it into discrete parts or react to it as a whole? Is it possible for you not to focus on the small details but to view yourself as a whole person? Why?

CHAPTER 4

The Dangers of Trying to Do the Impossible

O ne reason that the things we've been talking about are important is what can happen when somebody sets out to do the impossible. A girl decides that the way her body is made doesn't matter if she's willing to dedicate her energy to changing it. Or believes that she can remake herself into something other than who she is. Or thinks that if she can only get her body to look right everything else will be OK. This is the kind of thinking that can lead to an eating disorder such as anorexia or bulimia.

ANOREXIA

What is anorexia, anyway? And what's so wrong with trying to be real thin? Clinically speaking, anorexia is an eating disturbance that is marked by a body weight less than 85 percent of what is considered ideal for your height and bone structure, a distorted body-image, an intense fear of gaining weight, and (in females) the absence of menstrual periods.

Practically speaking, anorexia is a disorder in which the person attempts to control her world by controlling her food. She generally restricts her food intake severely with the goal of losing weight (and the belief that when she loses the weight she will feel better). Sometimes this process can make a person feel unnaturally wonderful. She's found it! She's thinner than anybody else and everybody notices it. They may say she's lost too much weight, but she is sure they're just jealous. I have had patients near starvation, with their bones literally poking through their skin, telling me how wonderful it is finally to look beautiful. And they're not kidding. They really see themselves this way. This euphoric response tends to occur when the disorder is new and the person is filled with the feeling of success, although it can persist for years.

For some, there is less euphoria and more of the feeling, "It still isn't good enough." For this girl, reaching her goal doesn't feel as good as she thought it would, so she continues to "diet" until she reaches what she considers a "safe" weight—a weight where she doesn't feel fat. When she awakens in the morning, the first thing she does is weigh herself. If she's under the magic number, it can be a good day. If she's not, the day is ruined even before it begins. And she can still feel "unsafe" at some very low weights—such as 60 or 70 pounds.

For others, there is no safe weight. They always feel

that if they were to gain even one pound they would immediately blow up to obesity. So they never get to rest, and they are never comfortable. In fact, in the process of trying to feel in control of their lives they have actually fallen prey to an unrelenting and demanding master.

One of the ways that this master holds sway is through distorted body-image. The anorectic sees herself much as she would look in a carnival mirror—heavy where there is no heaviness and big where there is no bigness. At an emaciated 75 pounds, she still feels fat and un-attractive and believes that she needs to lose even more weight. With this type of distortion operating, there is no relief. To give up the fight, for even one moment, could result in complete failure.

Or, at 75 pounds, she may not see fatness but she also may not be able to see her emaciated body with its look of wasting illness. She may only see someone who finally is more attractive. But, once again, the only way to keep this success is to continually deny what most of us accept.

One of the hallmarks of anorexia is how noble it can make the person feel. She is able to deny herself what the rest of us can't resist. That puts her a step above the crowd and gives her something that makes it all feel worthwhile—superiority. Many anorectics say that this is the hardest part of giving it up—it makes them or-dinary and causes them to lose their sense of specialness. Well, there's no denying the appeal of that—who doesn't want to feel special? But it seems important to look at the price tag on the feeling.

Anorexia can kill you. The mortality rate for the dis-order is estimated at about one in ten. That means that of every ten young women starving themselves to look better, one of them will die trying. One of the most common causes of death is heart failure, because starvation causes a loss of muscle and one of the vital muscles in the body is the heart. The body doesn't differentiate between the thigh and the heart when it is starving: It steals muscle so that it can live. But sometimes the heart is robbed too far and stops. Thus many girls who are trying to get just a little thinner or just a little bit more special are getting that much closer to killing themselves. It seems to me there must be a better way to feel good about yourself.

Other costs of anorexia are less dramatic than death. It can cause gastrointestinal problems, sensitivity to cold, fainting, and hair loss. But the side effects are not only physical in nature. When the anorectic restricts, she restricts more than food. She restricts everything. It's as though she draws a circle around herself and says, "Nothing that would nurture me can pass through here." Her world narrows to a single point of interest: weight and food. Nothing else matters. She doesn't take in positive messages from her environment. She no longer notices beauty around her. In many cases, when her weight is very low, her thinking becomes confused and unclear. She drops out of friendships because they interfere with what's most important—the rituals around food. She isolates herself from age-appropriate activities and functions. Friends may drop her because there's not much left in her to be a friend to. The anorectic girl restricts growth. She stops her body from moving toward emotional and physical maturity. She loses hips, breasts, and menstrual periods (that's another way her body tries to cut down on costs and help her survive).

Her body literally stops developing. It stays right where she wants it—away from anything that might make her grow up or become sexual. The anorectic defines the world very narrowly, and it has to do only with food and her body. That's what feels safe.

CINDY

Cindy was thirteen and the younger of two daughters. She lived with her mother and sister in a small town in the Southwest. Her parents had divorced when she was four years old, and she didn't see much of her father anymore. He had remarried and moved away, and he now made only sporadic phone calls on holidays or birthdays. She missed her father—at least, she missed her memories of him—but she didn't have much to say to the man who called her on the phone. Her mother liked her sister best—at least that's the way Cindy saw it. She seemed so friendly with her sister and so critical of her. Sometimes Cindy felt as if her mother blamed her for her father's leaving and the way her mother's life had turned out. She knew that was silly, but it seemed like it sometimes.

Cindy had never been heavy, but she had a stockier build than her sister, and at thirteen she had just started to have her body changes and was feeling heavier than ever. She decided to go on a diet. She started out by having big salads for dinner and just juice for breakfast and an apple for lunch. Her mother didn't mind, particularly since Cindy assumed the responsibility for making her own dinners. And she seemed easier to get along with since she started her diet.

Cindy was excited about the change she was making.

She felt that it was very important and was going to make a big difference in how she felt about herself. She began to lose weight, and this gave her the encouragement she needed to keep losing more. She began an exercise program to help her lose weight even more quickly.

She had never had many friends, but she slowly stopped having much to do with the few she had. Her grades in school were still all right, but she had stopped going to club meetings and always seemed in a hurry to get somewhere else. That somewhere else was usually home and exercise. Gradually she became preoccupied with keeping track of her calories and their expenditure. She developed rituals around mealtime and ate her food in a particular way. It seemed important to do it this way and made her feel safer. She also began to exercise even more, to the point where she worried her mother. If she were sitting down, she wiggled her feet to try to burn off a few more calories. She began to exercise in her bedroom with the door shut so her mother wouldn't know what she was doing. Increasingly, food and exercise became the focus of her life, all that really mattered to her.

Cindy weighed herself each morning before going downstairs for juice with ice in it. If she weighed less than 85 pounds (she was 5'2"), she felt good and had energy for almost anything. If she weighed 85 pounds or more, she felt ugly and disgusting and fat. On those days, she didn't even want to go to school; she didn't want people to see her looking so fat. Often she told her mother she had a stomachache; then she stayed home and didn't let herself have anything but water so she would lose the weight.

Cindy didn't know she was caught in a death trap. When she weighed less than 85 pounds, she felt better about herself than she could remember ever feeling before. When she weighed too much, it was her own fault that she didn't feel good and she knew what she had to do to feel better. Her mother nagged her about eating, but her mother had always nagged her about something. This was something that she could control. This felt like an improvement.

BULIMIA

Bulimia is another eating disorder that can result from trying to do the impossible. It is marked by the consumption of a large quantity of calories at one time, followed by a purge that may involve self-induced vomiting, laxatives, diuretics, excessive exercise, or strict dieting. Bulimics also have a distorted body-image. They tend to be heavier than anorectics, but they can have very low weight as well.

The bulimic wants to have her cake and eat it too. She wants to eat all that she craves, but she doesn't want to get fat. So—the perfect solution: Eat it, then lose it. But once again, the solution isn't so perfect. It turns out that the bulimic cycle can be just as demanding and controlling as the anorectic's. What began as something she elected to do becomes something she has to do. The binge-purge cycle often becomes a release that she finds nowhere else in her life; that pressure builds until she gives in to the need to consume calories and then throw them away. The purging, which once worked to keep weight off, stops working that way after a while. The body does its best to adjust to this strange situation. That may mean that she becomes afraid of getting fat and begins to restrict—only to find that her need to binge grows even greater. So the cycle continues.

Whereas the anorectic could feel noble, the bulimic is left with guilt and self-contempt brought about by her repeated weakness in the face of temptation—to binge and purge. Most bulimics are disgusted by their behavior (and believe that others would be too if they knew), so it becomes a dark secret that they must hide. And then the bulimic cycle becomes a way to handle their secret and how they feel about themselves.

Like anorexia, bulimia can kill and maim. The most common cause of death is heart failure because of an electrolyte imbalance caused by purging. Sometimes girls choke to death on their vomit. Sometimes they tear their esophagus by continually vomiting or lose part of their colon through the repeated misuse of laxatives. Generally the tooth enamel is eroded by the acid brought up with vomit, and many bulimics develop rotten teeth. All this in the name of beauty.

But the side effects are not limited to physical abuse. The bulimic often finds herself increasingly isolated as more and more of her life is consumed by the binge-purge cycle. There isn't time to see friends or do homework or develop outside interests. Her thoughts are always on food—what she will eat, when she will eat it, and how she will get rid of it. And since all this is a secret, she has to use a lot of energy hiding it. She often has to lie about where she's been, what she's been doing, where the money went, and so on. That gets in the way of developing good relationships with others. They stop trusting her, and she comes to trust only her food. So she turns increasingly to food for comfort, only to have to purge and then feel guilty, which leads her back to food for comfort. It's another no-win situation.

HEATHER

Heather was sixteen and next to the youngest of five girls in a family that lived in Utah. Her father was very successful and the family was quite wealthy. They were also Mormon and had very definite rules about how life was to be conducted. Heather adored her strong and outgoing father, even though he could be very difficult and demanding; but she had a somewhat lukewarm relationship with her mother, who was much more passive and subdued.

Heather had always been headstrong, wanting to do things in ways that did not meet her family's sense of propriety. Her father seemed to admire her spunk but also reprimanded her for her behavior. Her mother simply didn't understand her.

Heather's father prided himself on his appearance and expected his family to do the same. He occasionally suggested to Heather that she should be careful—she might be putting on a little weight. That always embarrassed and angered her. She couldn't help feeling ashamed that she looked heavy but was furious that her father would mention it. She would diet and lose weight, but it always came back and she had to start all over again.

The winter of her sixteenth year had been particularly difficult for her. She had just broken up with Danny, a boy whom she had dated for the past two years. He was someone she liked very much but someone her father did not like. She and her father had argued about Danny repeatedly, arguments that often resulted in her telling Danny that she couldn't see him anymore. Her father didn't approve of him, and Heather very much wanted her father's approval. Typically, the breakup would last a week or two, and then she and Danny would get back together again. This time, the breakup had lasted two months. Heather was miserable but determined to find another boyfriend.

Instead, she began to eat. And she began to put on weight. She felt trapped, with nowhere to turn. She didn't feel able to quit eating and couldn't bear to get fat. So she began to vomit after eating. They weren't really meals. They were just large amounts of the food she wanted, and when she'd eaten all she could, she threw it all up. She began to eat and purge more and more. On weekends she did as many as eight or ten cycles of binging and purging. On those days she often felt spaced out and numb. Other days she was able to save the binging and purging until the end of the day. Then she did it only two or three times.

She came to think of binging and purging as a companion. It was there whenever she needed it, and it never let her down. Sometimes it felt demanding—not unlike her father—but it kept her from experiencing all the painful feelings she had about losing Danny and endlessly trying to please her father, and it was quick and immediate. That it wasn't going anywhere didn't bother her. It was enough that it was here for her now.

Exercises

Do you have a "safe" weight? How do you feel about yourself if you're below that weight? How do you feel if

you're above it? Why? Does that make sense to you?
Would you like to change any of this? What would you
change? Maybe you should try a smaller step first.

Do you restrict yourself around food? Why? Are you
willing to do this for the rest of your life? At what age
would you be willing to be heavier? How would you look
if you didn't watch your weight so closely? Are you sure?

Do you recognize yourself in either the anorectic or
bulimic descriptions? Do you share any of their characteristics? Which ones? How do you feel about that?
Would you like to change it? Why?

Do you recognize people you know in the above descriptions? Does that surprise you? Do you think that
anorectic or bulimic behavior is widespread among
girls and women? What does that suggest to you? What
does it make you want to change? Why?

What if you didn't spend so much time worrying about
your weight? What would you use that time for? Which
of the two alternatives seems most helpful toward your
growth and development? Which is likely to leave you
stuck where you are? What decision do you want to
make?

CHAPTER 5

Too Much of a Good Thing

I want to give some special attention to the role that exercise has come to play in our society. In the past ten years or so we have become a nation of exercise worshipers, and the trend shows no signs of slowing down. It's hard to find someone who isn't exercising, or talking about exercising, or intending to exercise. And if they're not actually doing it, they're explaining how they need to start. We seem to believe that any exercise is inherently healthy, no matter what its motivation and no matter how much time it takes. But we're wrong. This failure to realize the potential dangers of exercise contributes to its widespread misuse. Many of us have begun to use exercise as more than a way to have fun or be healthy. We have begun to use it like an addiction—or like a drug.

HOW DO YOU KNOW
IF YOU'RE MISUSING?

Moderate exercise is an important part of a well-balanced life. For those who are training to develop athletic skills in a particular sport, more than moderate exercise is probably fine and appropriate. But there's a line (and it may be a fine one) that increasingly is crossed. When or where it's crossed isn't always clear, so each of us has to consider it carefully for ourselves. It has to do with using exercise as a way to compensate for excessive calories consumed, or as the primary avenue for experiencing self-acceptance, or as a substitute for other important things that aren't in your life and should be. Some people call this problem exercise abuse, some call it exercise compulsion, and some call it exercise addiction. No matter what you call it, it means trouble.

To think about your own exercise and whether or not you're misusing it, you can keep a number of questions in the back of your mind. How important is exercise to my feelings of self-esteem and self-worth? What role does it play in my life? Am I really using it in a health-promoting way? What priority does it have in my life?

Exactly when exercise becomes a problem is sometimes hard to detect. Its dangers become hidden by our culture's love affair with aerobics, jazzercise, nautilus, running, jogging, and just about anything else that moves you around. Advertising and the media say it's very important to work out and tone up and get in shape. And we all enjoy feeling healthier, stronger, and more powerful. But exercise can be used to hide problems that need looking at, or it can give us a false sense of self-esteem. It can block our growth and development as people and prevent us from discovering other important aspects of ourselves. How does this happen? Well, here's a possible scenario.

EXERCISE AS BEST FRIEND

Maybe you didn't have many opportunities to feel good about yourself before. Perhaps it was hard for you to feel success and accomplishment at school or in other areas of your life. But now, with exercise, you have a way to feel those things without having to involve others or needing their approval. You can just work out and feel good. What happens sometimes, though, is that with this newfound area for success other areas for accomplishment begin to drop out or take on less importance. Gradually, what you accomplish in exercise becomes more and more important as an indicator of whether or not you're OK. And there's the problem. It's not necessarily the exercise that's a problem (unless it's excessive) but what it has come to mean to you and what other things no longer mean.

Perhaps you decide to take up running. Just a couple of miles at first, but it develops into a longer and longer run—to the point where it takes a couple of hours. Maybe you begin to run every day after school and do even longer runs on the weekend. Perhaps you don't have a boyfriend or aren't as popular as you wish you were, but those things don't seem so important now that so much of your time is taken up with running. It feels good and you feel better. But what it doesn't do is let you practice your social relationships so that you can know yourself better and discover what you need in that realm. It keeps you preoccupied with your body and robs you of the chance to develop some of the skills you'll need to grow.

ANGIE

Angie was fourteen and a freshman in high school in a small town in the Midwest. She was shy and quiet; it was easy for her to be in a room and have nobody know she was there. She tended to keep to herself. She had a few friends, but no one particularly close. She didn't feel good, but she didn't feel real bad either. She didn't seem to feel much at all—just kind of drifted along.

In the spring, when track season started, Angie decided to try out because she thought it was a sport that she might be able to manage. She wasn't athletic and hadn't been able to play basketball, softball, or any of the other games that required skills she didn't have. She tried out, and she wasn't bad. The coach took her on but said she would really have to practice and work out if she wanted to be competitive. Angie took the coach at her word. She ran during after-school practice, and she ran after she got home. She ran Saturday and Sunday, even if there wasn't a meet. Pretty soon Angie was running more than she wasn't. She liked it. She liked the attention she got from the coach, who thought she showed a great "attitude." She liked the feeling of importance she had because she was on the team and was doing OK. And she liked the feeling of having a purpose. Before, she had never really felt that she belonged. Now, she was a "runner." She was on the team.

When the season was over Angie continued to run and practice. Throughout the summer she kept the same intense workout schedule and regarded running as the most important thing in her life. More and more, running was her constant companion. Without it, she felt empty; with it, she felt connected to something important. She avoided whatever interfered with her running—which meant just about everything. She no longer saw much of her friends and didn't really mind. Her field of vision had come to include running and only running. If she ran well, she felt good about herself. If she didn't, she could think only about what she had to do to run better.

EXERCISE AS DRUG

Another possible scenario is that you feel unhappy and depressed and don't really know why or what to do about it—a little like the people we've talked about throughout the book. Maybe you decide that what you need is more exercise. At first that may be a good idea, because moderate exercise is a good way to feel better when you're depressed. Perhaps you notice that you do feel a little better. You decide that if a little is good, more is better, so you increase the intensity and amount of your workout until it takes up more and more of your time. Maybe, without your even realizing, it becomes the most important thing in your day. Without it, you feel lethargic, unfocused, and unattractive. But after your workout you feel a kind of "high"—not unlike the effect of some drugs. You are probably experiencing your body's response to extreme exercise, a kind of natural drug that you produce under certain kinds of stress. It may be that you are medicating your depression with the natural pain relievers that your body produces during your workout. But the exercising is taking up most of your time, and if you skip a few days you feel miserable. It has become something you have to do in order to feel OK. Each and every day.

DONNA

Donna was sixteen and a junior in high school. Her family had moved to the Northeast after her father retired from the military. Her mother had family there, and her father had gotten a part-time job so that he could be semiretired. Donna hated moving, she hated the town, and she hated her new house. She didn't even really like the kids at school. They were different from her friends in Tennessee, where she had grown up, and she felt like odd-man-out with them. The school was much bigger than the one she had gone to before. It was just too much for her: too many new people, too many new ways of doing things, too many changes. She was depressed and tired and spent a lot of time in her room.

In the summer, when school was over and she began to have a little more energy, she decided to start an exercise program. Nothing flashy, just a way to tone up her body and look a little better. She found an exercise club that had classes every day and enrolled for the summer. At first she went three times a week. She was sore, but she also felt better than she had since she'd moved. She liked the instructors, and it was fun being with other people even if she didn't know them and they weren't friends. She felt competitive with some of the younger girls and was pleased that her body was beginning to look better than theirs. So she started going to class every day and felt even better. For one thing, she was looking better than she had in a long time, and she thought that maybe when school started she'd have better luck making friends. But even more important, she felt a real "rush" from her workout. At the end of class, she had a feeling that she could do almost anything. She had never experienced anything like it before. And with exercise she felt safe, almost as if it had become her lucky charm.

When school did start in the fall, Donna didn't have time for much besides studying and going to exercise class. She found that she didn't want to let up on the program. She tried doing less but didn't feel as good about herself. So when friends asked her to go to the library, or go to the mall, or anything else that would interfere with her workout, she had to say "No." It would mean missing a class, and she couldn't do that. Gradually, friends stopped asking. And, gradually, she felt less and less able to give the exercise up. It had become too important.

There are less extreme misuses of exercise. It doesn't have to become so time-consuming that you don't have room for anything else. Some people appear to be exercising normally, but if they were to stop or even cut down they would immediately feel unattractive, or out of control, or too heavy. For them, exercise maintains the very delicate balance between feeling acceptable and not. And that means that there are other places in their lives that need attention but likely won't get it while exercise does the trick.

JOAN

Joan was nineteen and worked as a secretary for a large insurance company in Boston. She had graduated from high school and gone straight to work. She didn't have the money for college and didn't see the point, anyway. She had never liked school that much and couldn't see asking for more.

Joan and three roommates shared a large apartment in a popular section of town. She had known these girls for years and they were good friends. They tended to do things together—go to movies or shop for clothes—and had become like family for one another. Lately two of her roommates had found steady boyfriends. It didn't really bother her—she had lots of friends—but sometimes she wondered when she'd meet "Mr. Right" and sometimes she worried that she might not. It was hard to see her roommates hooked up with their future and not know where her future might be.

Joan had joined a health club. She had always been a little heavier than she liked but had never seriously dieted or anything like that. When she first visited the club, the trainer who evaluated her said she needed to lose fifteen pounds and tone up.

She got right into it. She went three times a week and worked hard while she was there. And she loved going. Well, maybe not going, but she loved the way she felt when she left. She felt better about herself and liked the results she saw on her body. Other people noticed too. Men at work commented, and she felt prettier and more attractive than she had in some time.

The club became a part of her life-style. She went regularly as clockwork. It became like any other responsibility or necessity. And it really did make her feel better. But if for some reason she was unable to go she felt fat and uncomfortable. Without plugging into the fitness club, she didn't have the same feelings of self-acceptance and confidence. She knew she probably wasn't *really* fatter, but she sure felt it.

Exercises

The following are some important questions for assessing how you use exercise. If you recognize yourself on this list, you are likely misusing exercising.

1. Are your feelings of self-worth dictated by the frequency and intensity of your exercising?
2. If you go two days or more without exercising do you begin to feel anxious, guilty, unattractive, or out of control?
3. Do you continue to exercise even when it poses a risk to your health?
4. Are you tired from overexercise? Do you have trouble sleeping at night even though you are tired?
5. Does the extent of your exercising interfere with your social or school life? Do you back out of commitments because they might interfere with your workout?
6. Have you become secretive about the extent of your exercising?

Imagine that you are unable to exercise for the next two weeks, that something absolutely prohibits you from taking part in any exercise. What are your feelings? Are you scared? Are you surprised at the intensity of your response? What does that mean about you and exercise? What does it suggest you might want to do differently? Does it have to be all or nothing?

Add up all the time you spend around exercise in a given week. Include dressing for it, warming up, exercising, cooling down, and thinking about it. How many hours is it? Does that surprise you? What might you do with that time if you didn't exercise? What would be comfortable about that? Does this suggest anything to you?

CHAPTER ◇ 6

Trying to Be More
Than You Are

Although this book focuses largely on the female issues of dieting and the need to be thin, no book on negative body-image would be complete without looking—if only briefly—at the adolescent male's struggle for identity and self-acceptance. We've talked about how our culture asks its girls to be thinner and trimmer than most of them would be if left alone. What we haven't talked about is how many boys feel a cultural push to be bigger and stronger than they are. Boys, like girls, face adolescence with a compelling need to be acceptable. And while the dynamics that influence this pressure may differ from those directing females, they are still powerful.

The historical image of the strong male who can protect those around him still lingers. Men, in this culture, are expected to be many things, including powerful, confident, assertive, aggressive, large, strong, tall, handsome, athletic, sexual, and competitive. That's quite a checklist. How is a young boy, just entering puberty, to make the transition from what he's been to all that he's supposed to be? How is he to wade through the early years of adolescence, often feeling awkward and ungainly, while he waits for the magical male physique and mentality to settle on him? And what if they never do?

While we ask women to be too little, we ask men to be too much. And the boys who never seem to become mature men, even though their years suggest that it is time, are evidence of the impossible quest that we ask them to make. Comic books and TV shows and movies are filled with stories of males doing battle, overcoming impossible odds, saving the day and the damsel, and in any number of other ways being heroic figures. Superman was a wonderful image, but he was a comic book character, then a TV series and, finally, a movie star. He was never an honest-to-goodness man. He was, I suspect, a mixture of the dreams and fantasies of a culture that likes its men to be larger than life.

How does this cultural push to be big and physical and athletic and a winner affect boys who are on their way to adulthood? Well, if they are naturally big and strong, well built and athletically talented, the impact is probably less than if they are small, slight, not so well coordinated on the playing field, and slower to develop physically. For the latter group, the emotional scars and wounds may be such that they linger for life.

DAVID

David was fifteen and a sophomore in high school. He lived with his older brother and two younger sisters in a neighborhood outside of Philadelphia. His dad worked in construction, and his mom was pretty much a homemaker.

David was smarter than his brother, Jeff, and did better in school, but he was not the athlete that Jeff was. He was much smaller and lighter and not as quick in sports. When he'd been younger, none of this had mattered so much. But now that he was in high school it seemed very important. If you wanted to go out with the popular girls, you had to be on the football team or the basketball team or, at least, the baseball team. But the football team was best. And if you wanted to be accepted by the guys, you had to be good in sports. But David wasn't. He didn't have a chance. He simply didn't have the size you needed. Even some of the girls were taller and bigger than he was.

David began to feel embarrassed and ill at ease with his body. He was especially uncomfortable in the locker room where everybody paraded around. There was no privacy in the showers and no place to hide. Most of the boys left him alone, but some of the older guys laughed and made fun. Sometimes his brother stuck up for him, and sometimes he didn't.

David began to feel increasingly self-conscious about his body, which meant he was increasingly self-conscious about himself. He didn't go to parties sometimes because he just didn't feel good enough to go. He'd become anxious, and worry about what would or wouldn't happen, and eventually end up staying home. If he did go, he'd feel uncomfortable and end up not having a good time.

He kept working in school, because that was the only place he seemed to do well, but it didn't do much to help how he felt about himself. It was nice to get As, and his parents were proud of him, but that didn't impress girls and it even made him look like a squid. Gradually, David was more and more unhappy and found himself waiting for something to change—like for his body to become bigger and better overnight.

If David were around today, he could probably find a "solution" to part of his problem. Perhaps he couldn't get taller, but he could put on some bulk and add some strength. He could use anabolic steroids, the growing drug of choice in high schools and colleges to get a bigger, stronger body.

WHY STEROIDS?

What are steroids and why are people using them? They are chemicals similar to the male hormone testosterone. Originally developed in the 1930s to treat wasting diseases and anemia, they were later used to combat the negative side effects of cancer treatments. A new use emerged in the 1950s, however, when the East German athletes using synthetic testosterone began to dominate the strength-related Olympic events. By the late 1960s steroids had become common equipment among world-class athletes. Like most fads, this one has now trickled down to the rest of us. An estimated one million Americans use steroids. These are not just adults; they are not just males, either, but they are primarily male.

The activities most likely to lead boys to steroids are football, wrestling, swimming, and track and field events that emphasize upper-body strength. But not only athletes are using them. Steroids are finding a most promising niche in the health clubs, where boys who simply want to be bigger and more muscular see them as a natural partner. A large and well-organized black market ensures that a supply is available where boys work out, where they hang out, and where they go to school. Steroids can now be bought from the same dealer who sells you all your other drugs.

There's no doubt about it, steroids deliver. When used in conjunction with a high-calorie diet and a weight-training program, they build muscle mass and strength. Users tend to train harder and become stronger more quickly, and they often develop feelings of euphoria and heightened self-esteem. Not bad. Not bad, at all. But there's a price, and it's high. Most kids using steroids do so without medical supervision and use more than the recommended dosage. The potential long-term dangers of this type of misuse include kidney damage, cardiovascular disease, stroke, liver tumors, stunted growth, weakened tendons, prostate and liver cancer, and even death. The less serious physical effects include acne, jaundice, a puffy face, swelling of the feet and legs, changes in the male reproductive system (smaller testicles, low sperm count, increased sex drive), and darkening of the skin.

The psychological effects are every bit as troubling. Heavy steroid users can show signs of "bodybuilder's psychosis," with symptoms ranging from delusions of grandeur to paranoia to hearing voices. Others may suffer from serious mood disturbances such as mania or severe depression, or experience attacks of anxiety. Most users, even when their use is less extreme, report that they become more violent. They feel pumped-up and need to do something with this aggressive energy. If they're on the football team, they may want to injure the player they tackle. If they're at a party and drinking, they may want to hurt somebody who looks at them the wrong way. If they're with their girlfriend, they may become violent with her. If there's a gun nearby, they may want to use it.

Users also report that steroids are hard to give up. If you feel pumped-up and great on them, you are likely to feel depressed and listless when you try to stop. Once you're in the circle, it's hard to get out.

MATT

Matt was eighteen and a junior in high school. His family lived in a nice section on the outskirts of Cleveland, and he and his younger sister attended the local high school, which had a particularly strong football program. Matt had been on varsity since he was a sophomore. He hadn't started last year, but he was a natural athlete and the coach had been impressed. The coach liked to get the boys with talent and teach them early so that by their senior year they were well in the saddle. Matt was good, but he could be better. He needed to be bigger, and he needed a little more of the "killer instinct."

During the summer before his junior year, Matt had begun working out more and trying to add bulk to his frame. It had made him a little bigger, but not a lot, and he had become discouraged by the apparent limitations on what he could become physically. He knew that some of the guys used "roids" to help develop strength, but he wasn't a drug user and wasn't willing to run the risk of the possible side effects. When the school year started he was still committed to playing "naturally," but he didn't get played much. The coach said he wasn't working hard enough and chose the bigger players to start. Matt was spending more time on the bench than on the field. He felt discouraged and frustrated and a failure. He had to do something. The other guys didn't seem to be bothered by any side effects—and they were playing.

The pills were easy to come by. In fact, the guys joked that they'd known he'd give in and had been saving some for him. The change was dramatic. It was as though his muscles swelled overnight. He felt like the Hulk. He didn't get as sore from the workouts, and he had more energy. The coach noticed the difference and began to play him more, and he played well. He felt different on the field, more aggressive and powerful, and he didn't hold anything back. It was wonderful and he felt as good as he ever had.

As the season progressed, he was using more and really building up his body. He had put on a lot of weight and looked very different. His mother commented on the change but assumed he was just working out extra hard. His father expressed surprise, saying he'd never looked like that when he played ball. But nobody asked him about using steroids.

Matt developed acne on his chest and back but figured that this was just another side effect of being a teenager. His girlfriend noticed that he was becoming increasingly moody, but she thought it must be the pressure of school and football and the intense weight training he was doing. But the mood swings grew worse. Sometimes he would be sweet and gentle and sometimes mean and violent. His parents began to talk about him as Dr.

Jekyll and Mr. Hyde, and they began to worry that something was really wrong. But Matt thought everything was fine. He was playing ball, and he was bigger than he'd ever been. He wasn't going to give up roids just because his parents and his girlfriend were having a hard time with him. Besides, he had tried to cut down when a TV show on steroid abuse had scared him, and he'd felt horrible without them.

SIMILAR YET DIFFERENT

It is likely that some of the forces that push girls into eating disorders and preoccupation with body and weight operate to propel boys along the path of bodybuilding and steroids. If you're a boy, you might look at the next couple of chapters to see how they apply to you. Certainly family functioning, comfort level with feelings, and thinking styles affect all of us. Issues of poor self-esteem and feelings of inadequacy are bound to send both boys and girls to the well of body improvement. But by and large our culture still gives boys more room to "act" and asks girls simply to "appear."

Exercises

What do you think are the characteristics of the ideal American male? Which of them do you possess? Which would you like to possess? Is that realistic? Could you be content without some? Which ones? Why? What does this mean for you?

How do you feel about your body's size and strength? How likely is it that you will develop more bulk and strength? What does that say about what goals are realistic for you? What goals are unrealistic? How far would you go to reach the unrealistic ones? Why? What does that suggest about your relationship with yourself? Would you like to change that?

If you could be a football star in high school right now but knew that you would have to pay with your long-term health and possible emotional problems, what would you choose to do? Why? What does that say about your priorities? What does it say about your long-range view? What does it say about the care you are willing to show yourself? Want to change any of this? Why?

CHAPTER 7

What Does Your Family Have to Do with It?

ROLES AND EXPECTATIONS

Families are fascinating places. They are where we are born and learn about ourselves and the world around us. To a very large extent they are responsible for the form we take and our view of the world. That is not to say that we aren't born with certain tendencies to be this way or that. But these tendencies generally become muted or exaggerated depending upon the encouragement or dampening they get from those around us.

To complicate this process, the way our parents see us and treat us is largely a function of who they are and how their family saw and treated them. No matter who you are or what qualities you possess, your parents themselves possess a certain readiness to see you in a particular way or to have certain expectations about you. Some parents have more of the blanks left open than others and can give their children more room for self-expression. But some are less able to do this. You may know parents who expect or need their daughter to be "the most popular" or "the brightest in the class" or the "star gymnast." Sometimes there is a good fit between who the person is and what her parents need her to be. When that happens, she is able to be herself and meet her parents' needs at the same time. Maybe she wouldn't push for it so hard without parental pressure, and she probably resents it to some extent, but she is generally able to feel accepted for who she is and to get on with the task of growing up.

The real difficulty arises when a person doesn't have the qualities that would let her be what her parents need her to be. Or when she begins to feel that if she isn't this or that, she is nothing or a failure. Or maybe she feels that she will be loved and valued only if she becomes what her parents push her to be. When a person feels these things, she stops growing along her true path. She can't grow as herself because the person she is isn't valued. But she can't grow as what her parents want her to be because that isn't who she is or where her real growth would come from. So she's stuck and unable to move forward. At some level she knows it, but probably all she is aware of is that something is wrong and it feels as if it must be something that is wrong with her. Maybe she feels a kind of depression and wishes she were more popular. Maybe she thinks she'd feel better if she made better grades or better friends. Or maybe she decides that the reason she feels uncomfortable and uneasy with herself is because she's fat.

Perhaps her parents don't need for her to be out-standing; they may just need her to fill a certain role. Now, all families do this to some extent. They assign roles to their members according to such criteria as personality type, birth order, resemblance to someone else, and so on. The problem develops when the as-signed role doesn't leave room for the person who fills it. Perhaps as the "Baby in the Family" she isn't allowed to grow up. Or maybe as the "Responsible One" she is not allowed to make mistakes or must always be organized and on time. Or maybe as the one who is "Just Like Her Mother" she is not allowed to develop those aspects of herself that are very different from her mother. When the assigned role is too tight it feels uncomfortable and stops growth. But, once again, she may not be quite sure where the discomfort is coming from. All she knows is that she doesn't feel good about herself. Maybe she decides that it's her body, that she's too fat. Ah. That makes it simpler. Now all she has to do is lose weight.

ELIZABETH

Elizabeth was thirteen and the youngest of four children. It had always been whispered that she had been an after-thought or even a mistake. She was ten years younger than her sister, and her brothers were twelve and thirteen years older than she. Sometimes Elizabeth felt like an only child and wished that she had a sister closer to her age with whom she could be friends. She was close to her mother and did a lot of things with her like shopping and going to the mall, but it wasn't the same. Her mother always told her what to do and how to do it and never really let her make decisions by herself. That

doesn't mean that she didn't really love her mother—
she did. It was just that she sometimes wished she had a
little more room. Sometimes she felt that her mother
held her a little too tight. But she didn't want to hurt her
mother's feelings—after all, her mother always called
her "my sweet sunshine"—so she didn't say anything.
And, to be honest, she really depended on her mother
for her opinions and advice—even if she didn't want
them sometimes.

At the end of her thirteenth year, Elizabeth began to
feel ugly and unattractive and dissatisfied with herself.
She decided to go on a diet and try to look better. Her
mother always went on diets, but they never seemed to
work. Elizabeth decided to go on one and make it work.

She started out trying to lose ten pounds and exercise
three times a week. At first it was fun and something her
mother supported. Gradually she lost the ten pounds,
but it didn't feel like enough. Eventually, Elizabeth
became more secretive about what she was and wasn't
eating, and her mother became less happy with her
dieting. It became something that they battled about.
And the battling became something that, in a funny way,
made Elizabeth feel good. She felt as though her diet
and food intake had become one area where she made
the decisions and her mother couldn't interfere. She felt
better about herself now that she was thinner. She felt
that she was finally growing up.

FAMILY RULES

Sometimes families have very strict rules about what's
allowed and what's not allowed. Once again, all families
do this, but in some families the rules restrict the kinds

of things that all of us need in order to be healthy. Such as "You're not allowed to get angry." Or "You must always be good." Or "You must always think as we do." Or "You have to stay young and not grow up." Or "You have to be sick so that we can focus on your illness and not on the other things that trouble us." These rules can feel pretty restrictive, but they are made even more difficult because they're unspoken. Generally, nobody says them out loud. That would probably be difficult, but at least you would know what was going on. But usually in a family with these kinds of rules nothing is said up front. You just feel them. You just know them, but not the way you know the rules of a game you're playing. You usually know them in your stomach.

Let's imagine that a rule in your family is that anger isn't allowed. You notice that it doesn't feel safe when people raise their voices. Your mother looks uncomfortable when you start to get upset. Your father withdraws and gets distant if you start to yell about something. So pretty soon you understand. Sort of. You begin to think it's not right for people to get angry, and so when you have angry feelings you feel guilty and uncomfortable. Then, if you get real good at it, you even stop knowing when you're angry; it all happens way below the surface so you don't have to feel bad about it. But at some level, you still do, and at some level you believe there's something wrong with you.

JULIE

Julie was seventeen and had lived in California all her life. She loved the good weather and all the things it let you do outside. She had always been fairly weight-conscious—everyone in her family was—and she watched what she ate pretty carefully. But her active life-style seemed to help her stay thin, and she had never been on a real diet.

Julie was an only child, and her parents had been in their forties when she was born. Growing up, she had always heard how much they had wanted her and how long they had tried to have her. She had been born prematurely, and her parents had worried about her constantly. As she had grown older, they had always been a little overprotective. Julie hadn't been allowed to do a lot of things other kids did, but she had never minded it much. Mom always said it was because they loved her so much, and everybody told her how lucky she was to have such neat parents who bought her nice things and who always seemed so pleasant. Nobody in Julie's house was ever angry. She had never heard her parents yell at each other or fight, and they didn't get angry with her. Everybody just seemed to get along.

Until her junior year. Suddenly it seemed as if her parents were becoming even stricter. Julie and her friends were driving, and it was a time when she began to want more freedom. But her parents seemed to be making more restrictions rather than less. Julie tried to talk about her frustration, but her parents were unwilling to compromise. They just said "No" and expected her to forget about it and be fine again. But she wasn't. She began to have feelings about her parents that made her uncomfortable. She felt angry, but when she tried to talk about it and her voice got loud, her mother's lips would tighten and she would say, "That's enough." When she tried to argue with her father, he became very quiet and told her the conversation was over.

Julie felt unhappy and frustrated and found herself eating more. That was fine in the beginning, because it made her feel better, but then she began to notice that she was gaining weight. This frightened her, and she tried to cut back on what she was eating. She tried to be very strict with herself and not give in to temptation, but it didn't work. She began to think of food all the time and plan what she would "treat" herself to when she got home from school and before her parents got home from work.

One afternoon, after she had eaten a particularly large amount, she panicked and ran to the bathroom to try to vomit the food back up. It worked. All the food that she had just enjoyed eating was there in the toilet. She couldn't believe it—it was too good to be true. In fact it was, but she didn't know that then. She thought she had found a way to eat all the foods she had ever wanted and not gain weight. And she found that her preoccupation with food, the intrigue involved in eating and vomiting without her parents finding out, and her increasingly guilty feelings about what she was doing took the spotlight off the struggle she was having with her parents.

FAMILY SECRETS

Sometimes families have secrets about things that they pretend aren't true or didn't happen. They don't usually all get together and agree to pretend this thing. Once again, it's usually unspoken. But it's real. Maybe the thing they pretend is that even though Mom drinks a lot and gets really angry when she's drunk, she isn't an alcoholic. You and the others in your family don't talk about her "tendency to drink too much sometimes." You just notice how much tension there is in the air when she makes herself a drink.

Maybe Dad is physically abusive to you and the other kids and sometimes leaves bruises or worse. That's a secret; you don't talk about it in your family, and you're not supposed to tell anybody outside the family. It's your family's business and nobody else's, and to tell anybody and ask for help would be disloyal. So you lie when people ask you about an injury. But you can't help wondering why Mom doesn't make him stop, and it sure makes you scared to see him come home angry because that's when he's most likely to get into one of his "moods."

Maybe your father comes into your bedroom at night and fondles you. You can't tell your mother because she might be angry with you for letting it happen. Although, it's funny but sometimes you're sure she knows and is just pretending that she doesn't. But you can't ask her. Maybe you think it might be happening to other kids in the family, but you can't ask them either. It's supposed to be a secret, and it's too shameful and embarrassing to let anyone else know about it. You try to pretend it isn't happening and hope that it will stop, but you can feel your body stiffen whenever you pass your father in the hall.

Perhaps one of your parents is having an affair. Maybe your mother has had a boyfriend for some time, and it's a serious relationship. Your father knows about it, you and the other kids know about it, but no one says anything to anybody. Your family has decided, without any discussion, to handle this problem silently. So you worry about the consequences of her relationship and perhaps are angry with her for having the affair or angry with your father for not stopping it. Or maybe you're confused about how such a thing can happen. But you're not allowed to talk about it, even though people in the community may know about it and be talking about it a great deal. You and your family walk around the elephant in the living room and pretend it isn't there.

Sometimes the secrets aren't as clear as the ones I've described. Sometimes they're things that you don't even have an actual awareness of. But they can be real and powerful in affecting how your family thinks about itself, how you're allowed to behave, and what you're allowed to become. And we all know by now how easy it can be for a girl who's feeling uncomfortable to turn to food and her body to feel better.

JENNIFER

Jennifer was seventeen and the oldest of five children. She was very responsible, did well in school, and was a big help to her mother with the other kids. Her family didn't have much money, so Jennifer had a part-time job at a drugstore to help out. Sometimes she felt there wasn't enough time and energy to do all the things she tried to do, but she thought it was her responsibility to do them.

Her mother was a fairly quiet woman whose life revolved around her children and taking care of the home. She believed that a husband should make most of the decisions about the big things that affected the family, but she ran the house day-to-day.

Jennifer's father did construction work and was most comfortable working with his hands and least comfortable talking about feelings. He had a quick temper and got angry easily. If he had stopped off for a "couple of beers" on the way home from work, he could become violent. He did not hit Jennifer's mother, but he did hurt his children.

He was most violent toward Jennifer's younger brother, Brian. Jennifer wavered between feeling grateful and guilty that it was Brian who took the brunt of her father's anger. As crazy as it sounded, she somehow felt responsible for Brian's beatings, as though she should be able to protect him. But nobody protected him; nobody protected any of them. It never occurred to Jennifer to report the abuse to someone outside her family. It was something that she hoped would stop if only they were good enough or quiet enough or enough of whatever it took.

Jennifer had always felt different from other kids. Certainly she believed that what went on in her family didn't happen in other families. When she heard the kinds of complaints most kids had about their parents, she felt very old. In her senior year things escalated. Her mother was sick a lot, and Jennifer had to do more of the housework. She also had more responsibilities at school because she was class secretary. By the end of the day Jennifer felt depleted, and she began to eat large "snacks" at work before going home. At first it was something she did most days. Gradually, it became something she did every day and looked forward to during the day. She was scared when she began to gain weight and even more scared when she realized she couldn't stop the eating. One day at work she passed by the laxative section and decided to try using them to get rid of the food.

It worked. She felt more comfortable eating knowing

that she could get rid of the food later, and there was something about the use of laxatives that felt unexpectedly comfortable, even though it sometimes gave her stomach pains. It became an important part of the ritual of eating. Since the continual use of laxatives was expensive, she began to steal them from the store. Increasingly, her thoughts were with food, its elimination, and her fear of being caught stealing, rather than with her family and her multitude of feelings about it.

THERE'S NO PERFECT FAMILY

Let me talk just a bit more about families before we leave this section. Sometimes we think there's something wrong with our own family because it doesn't resemble the families that we see on popular television shows. But TV families are idealized; they have the luxury of a script writer who only lets those things happen that he or she knows how to fix in the end. Real life doesn't work that way. Real people come with different histories and with different emotional and intellectual resources.

All families have problems. There isn't one that doesn't. All families have strengths and weaknesses, and they're not the same for each family. For example, one family might not allow the expression of anger, but it also won't tolerate physical abuse. Another family might allow its members all kinds of freedom, but its members don't learn to respect limits. Yet another family might look "perfect" to outsiders but not give its members room to have flaws and make mistakes. Each of these strengths or weaknesses will influence its members in a different way.

If your family does not allow the expression of negative feelings and expects its members always to look well, you may become somewhat rigid and perfection-istic in your behavior. If, on the other hand, your family tends to let all feelings fly, with one member often talking for another, or has inconsistent rules, you are more likely to have trouble learning to be contained and structured and to operate within limits.

There is no perfect family. Even if the family down the street looks perfect, they're not. The trick is to come to understand your own family and to understand the role you play and its impact on you.

Exercises

What is your "role" in your family? How do you feel about it? Have you known it all along? Would you like to change it? Why?

What does your mother need you to be? Why? What does your father need you to be? Why? Is this all right with you? What does it mean you cannot become or do? What does it require you to do? Do you want to change any of this? Why?

What are the unspoken rules in your family? Whom or what do they protect? Why? What would happen if you broke them? What will happen to you if you don't? What does this make you want to keep the same and change?

Does your family have a secret or something that they pretend? Why? How far back does it go? Whom or what does it protect? Why? What is its impact on you? Do you want to keep this secret as it has been kept? What would that keep you from doing or let you begin to do?

Think about the type of family you live in. Is it restrictive or loose, abusive or overcontrolled, accepting or critical? When you've got a sense of your family, try to think of the type of person such a family would produce. Do you recognize yourself at all? Do you understand yourself a little better? What difference will this make to you? Why?

CHAPTER 8

Feelings, Anyone?

What are feelings anyway? I think of them as our immediate and naturally occurring response to something. It can be to something we see, hear, or feel. It can be to something that happened long ago, is happening now, or will happen in the future. But the thing that's best about feelings is that they just are. Very simple and straightforward. You don't have to work on them. They'll just naturally emerge. Unless—unless you start to fool around with them. Then it can get complicated. Sometimes people we live with start telling us *how* we should feel or *what* we should feel or *when* we should feel. This approach has never made any sense to me because it's contrary to the whole notion of what feelings are, but there's a lot of it going around.

Some people will tell you that you "should" feel something: You should love a particular person or you should like a particular food. Some people will tell you that you "shouldn't" feel something: You shouldn't be angry with your mother or you shouldn't like a particular boy. Some people will tell you that you should be happier or that you shouldn't be so sad. Or they'll tell you that you shouldn't be frightened, that it's a silly thing to be; or you should feel more confident, that it's the proper way to feel. But none of this makes any difference in how or what we feel. It only changes our relationship with our feelings. Now we can feel bad about how we feel. Now we can feel guilty because we have certain feelings. Makes you wonder whose feelings these are, anyway?

GLORIA

Gloria was thirteen and in the eighth grade. She was the oldest of three girls and lived with her family on a large ranch in Texas. Her father spent most of his time working the ranch and was never happier than when he was working with his hands or riding. He had grown up on this ranch and had never thought about doing anything else. Her mother had grown up in the East and had met her father while they were in college. As her mother put it, "I just fell madly in love, and if he was going to live on a ranch, I figured I was too." But she didn't enjoy it as her husband did, and sometimes she really missed the life she'd known as a girl. She had "spells" when she felt particularly blue and out of place, and during those times she would drink more than usual.

Gloria and her sisters were a year apart. Her father called them the "three stairs." It was hard for Gloria because she was treated just like the other two. She rarely got special privileges for being older. She had the same bedtime as the younger ones and the same rules about where she could go and what she could do. She resented it, but her mother told her she shouldn't feel that way, that she was lucky to have sisters to play with—luckier than her mother, who was an only child. Gloria hated it when her mother went on about how lucky she was. She didn't feel lucky. She felt mistreated.

The other hard part about her sisters was that they played with all her things, and came into her room without asking, and generally didn't respect her privacy. But anytime Gloria complained to her parents, her mother said that she was being silly and her father didn't seem to hear the complaint.

Gloria felt unheard and dismissed in other ways. Whenever she had a fight with a friend, her mother would say fighting was a waste of time and she should make up. When she asked for something special for Christmas, and it was the only thing she really wanted, she didn't get it. Her mother thought she was too young for that present and gave her something else—something like what her sisters got. There just seemed to be a steady stream of these kinds of experiences, and Gloria grew steadily more unhappy.

Everyone in her family was a little heavy. There was always lots of good food around, and her father loved a big dinner at night. In the middle of her eighth-grade year Gloria decided to go on a diet. She had put on some extra weight since the beginning of the year and thought she'd feel better if she got rid of the extra pounds before they became permanent. She started out with a goal of losing five pounds. She decided to skip breakfast and lunch and just eat dinner, but she didn't want the dinner her mother made. She decided to make the kind of dinner she wanted—a much lighter one.

It was easier than she had thought it would be. Sometimes she felt lightheaded from not eating in the morning, but she started sucking on Lifesavers to help her feel more energetic. And dinner was a dream. She fixed what she wanted and ate it by herself in the kitchen while everyone else chowed down on that heavy food. She didn't even miss being with them at dinnertime. It felt good to be by herself doing what she wanted.

The thinner she got, the better she felt. Her mother voiced concern that she was getting too thin, but Gloria dismissed it as just another example of her mother's not understanding. Her father wondered if maybe she was taking this dieting thing too far. She didn't think he understood either. All she knew was that she felt more special and successful than she ever had before. She didn't care how much willpower or self-control it took, she wasn't going to lose what she'd won. And the fact that it had become just about all she thought about didn't bother her at all.

KEEPING CLEAR ABOUT FEELINGS

When we're very young, we're usually quite clear about our feelings. If something's wrong, we cry. If something's right, we smile or coo. It's instant. A baby's face reflects feelings immediately and without censorship. Because nobody has yet had the chance to let her know she shouldn't or should. She just does.

Now I'm not recommending that we all become like babies—but maybe we could learn from them. Maybe we could let ourselves recognize and accept our feelings and then decide what we want to do with them. Maybe we could recognize feelings as important conveyors of information about who we are and what we need and then decide if we want to act on them. Feelings don't disappear just because you don't like them or think you shouldn't be feeling them. They are there and if rejected simply go underground where you have less control over them. But they don't go away.

KARLA

Karla was angry with her friend, Margie, because Margie had promised to do something with her on Saturday night and had apparently forgotten. Margie hadn't even let her know that something had come up so she'd have to back out. She had simply let Saturday come and go without calling. Karla felt hurt and angry, but she also felt silly for feeling that way. After all, this was the first time Margie had done such a thing, so why make a big deal about it? She didn't think she should feel as upset as she did, so she didn't say anything.

But when she saw Margie at school on Monday she didn't feel like being friendly. She wasn't mean to her—she just pretended she hadn't seen her.

Margie saw Karla look at her and then walk away. She couldn't understand what was going on. They hadn't had a fight—they hadn't even had a disagreement. She hadn't seen Karla since Friday afternoon when they'd talked about possibly doing something on Saturday. But her mother had wanted her to baby-sit so she hadn't done anything with anybody. Why was Karla being weird with her now? Margie couldn't figure it out. She knew that Karla could be moody sometimes. Maybe that was it. Well, she could just be moody; Margie wasn't going to get into it.

Karla was upset that Margie hadn't come after her. She knew that Margie must have seen her in the hall. Why hadn't she run after her? Well then, forget Margie.

*   *   *

This demonstrates how confusing things can get when someone doesn't honestly accept her feelings. Let's take a look at it. Karla tried to make light of her feelings of anger and disappointment because she felt they were silly and didn't think she should be feeling them. So she tried to hide them and pretend they weren't there. Of course, she communicated them indirectly, but since the message was indirect, her friend didn't know what she was saying. She made some guesses, but she couldn't be sure, and so she started to feel annoyed too. All this because Karla didn't feel entitled to be upset with someone and tell her so face-to-face. Looks to me as if that would have been a whole lot easier on everyone concerned.

But there's another cost to not allowing yourself to feel your feelings. It feels crummy. Holding a lot of angry feelings inside is highly uncomfortable, and pretending to feel happy when you're not feels false. Even worse, you run the risk of reaching a point of not knowing how you do feel about things. Well, if feelings are part of the rudder we use to guide us, that puts you at a real disadvantage. Now you don't know where you need to go, and just about no place feels right because you're so disconnected from yourself. Sometimes this snowballs so that as you become less and less able to steer yourself, you become more and more dependent upon others to tell you how to feel. Well, you may have already anticipated me. But it follows that if you feel unhappy and don't know why but want to do something to change things but don't know what—a ready place to go is on a diet. Maybe the problem is that you don't look right. Maybe if you were thinner you'd feel better. Maybe if your thighs weren't so big you'd have more self-confidence. Well, you'll fix that.

LAURA

Laura was eighteen and a senior in high school. She had an older brother who had been two years ahead of her and was the "perfect" son. He was handsome, smart, outgoing, and always had lots of girlfriends. Laura was not quite so perfect. She was somewhat pretty, did fairly well in school, and was shy and didn't date much. When she did go out, she tended to date boys who were like her—on the periphery of the popular groups.

Laura had spent most of her childhood in the West, but after her parents had divorced when she was nine her mother had moved with the children to a large town in North Carolina. Laura didn't see much of her father anymore. He had been something of a "drinker" and, although successful in business, was not very dependable in other ways. He often forgot her birthday or sent Christmas presents in February.

Laura felt insecure and uncomfortable with herself most of the time. She tried to handle these feelings by taking care of others and trying to please, but sometimes it felt exhausting and as if she was on a tightrope that might give way at any moment. She didn't understand how her brother could be so self-confident and popular. She wondered if maybe he'd gotten something you were supposed to get that she had missed. She noticed that he drank a lot, but so did lots of boys, and he never came home drunk or got into trouble that way.

She and her brother were not particularly close. They never talked about anything important—such as how they felt about the divorce or how things had been before her father left. She sometimes wondered if she had imagined the scenes of violence between her father and brother—or the uncomfortable feelings she had experienced sometimes when he used to ask her to sit on his lap. Nobody else ever talked about these things. Her mother tended to focus on the "positive" and encouraged her to "put the past behind her." One of her mother's favorite sayings was, "Negativity never solved anything."

It was during her senior year that Laura started to feel out of control. She had always worried about her body, but now she began to feel really fat. Disgustingly fat. And she hated the way her clothes looked on her. Her grades began to fall, and she didn't feel that she could do any better. She felt anxious and uncomfortable almost all the time and didn't know what to do about it.

So she decided to do something about what she could. She went on a diet. At least she could look decent. At first it worked. She lost some weight and didn't feel so unattractive. It was easier to go to school when she didn't hate herself. But the dieting was hard for her. It increased the tension she felt most of the time. So she started to set a goal for herself. If she was really good and dieted all week, she could have some of the things she wanted on the weekends. At first that worked. But eventually the weekends became an out-of-control frenzy of eating. And the dieting during the week wasn't enough to keep her from gaining weight. So, in a last-ditch

effort, she began to vomit after eating on the weekends.
And it quieted things for a while. At least she wouldn't
get fat, and that seemed like the most important thing of
all.

HARD TO SAY "NO"

Before I leave feelings, I want to talk briefly about the
word "No." It is remarkable how many girls and women
do not feel entitled to use the word. It's as though it
were a dirty word in some way. It must not pass their
lips. Now the word "Yes," it flows through their lips like
water. But "No"? Not in a million years. Why is that?
How can we make sense of it?

I think it comes, in part, from the way females are
traditionally raised—to please. To be sensitive to others'
feelings and not to offend. To take care of others and be
careful with them. To take a good deal of their self-liking
from the liking they receive from others. Taken to
extremes, this could produce a person who can't say
anything that might upset another and is *completely*
dependent upon that other for her own sense of self-
esteem. That's a pretty vulnerable position and a pretty
passive and acquiescent one too. What happens if someone asks her to do something she doesn't want to do?
Too bad. She not only does it, but she does it with a
smile. What if someone treats her in a way she doesn't
like? Too bad. She lets them do it and smiles while it
happens. What if someone expects something of her
that she doesn't want to do? Too bad. She tries hard to
do it and smiles in the trying. What do you imagine this
might do to a person? First of all, I think it would make

her feel very helpless and powerless. Second, I think it would make her feel trapped. Third, I think it would make her very angry.

The final point about not being able to say "No" is that your "Yes" can't really mean anything if you aren't able to say its alternative. "Yes" has meaning only if it is a real choice and the option of "No" is always present. I never feel that I can trust someone who can't tell me "No," because I never know if her "Yes" really means what she's saying or if it means she can't tell me otherwise. Then I have to worry about whether she really means it and say things like, "Are you sure?" It's much harder to know what's going on that way. Much easier when people have the whole range of responses to choose from and are able to pick according to how they feel.

Exercises

What feelings are you entitled to? Make a list of those feelings. What feelings are you not entitled to? Make a list of those. What do you feel when you look at the two lists side by side? Do you want to change either of the lists? Why?

Practice saying "No" five different times this week. Is it hard? Is it scary? What are you afraid of? Is that realistic? How do you feel when you say "No"? Is that realistic? Can you do it? Why? Do you want to change it? Are you sure?

What do you think happens to the feelings you don't let yourself feel? Where do you store them in your body? What does that part of your body feel like? Can you imagine letting it feel different? What would you need to do for that to happen? Is that OK? Why?

What do you think is the natural range of human emotions? Make a list of all the possible feelings you can think of. How many of them are you entitled to feel? Why? What does that do to you? How do the forbidden ones come out? Do you want to change this at all? Why?

CHAPTER 9

How to Keep a Bad Situation Going

AN INTERPERSONAL MODEL FOR SELF-ESTEEM

How does a girl keep herself feeling unacceptable and unattractive? How does she stay depressed and unhappy and feeling that the only answer is to focus on her body and try to make it better? How does she manage to distort her self-view so that she can always feel unsatisfactory?

We all have times when we feel depressed, dissatisfied with how we have done something, or just generally unhappy with ourselves. These feelings are part of the human landscape, and we all pass through them on our way to or from other locales. But some people are able to inhabit this part of the terrain exclusively. How do they do it? Before we explore how they can sustain such poor self-esteem, let's look at how we create our self-image in general.

We've already discussed the Self-esteem Bank and how people draw on accounts to feel better about themselves. Another model for thinking about this is an interpersonal one. According to this approach, people put things out and take things in from the world around them. When the system is working, information flows from the person to the world and back. What you put out has something to do with what you get, and what you take in has something to do with what you give. It's an interactive system that is able to make shifts and changes both inside you and out depending on what information is passing through. That means that you can let others know your limits and boundaries and respond to theirs, and you can receive information that tells you that you're wonderful or that you need to change something. This system lets you act on your environment as you need to and lets the environment act on you. When it's working well, it's a system of positive and negative influences that operates both ways.

But what if the system isn't working as it should? What if it only lets the person give out positive information and take in negative? What if the system doesn't let her receive positive information about herself and won't allow her to put out negative? What would a person feel like with a system that worked like that? Probably like a lot of girls—depressed, uncomfortable, and generally unhappy. However, a girl with a system that works like that usually doesn't know it's broken. She thinks *she* is. She doesn't know that she feels so crummy because her intake and output don't work. She believes she feels the way she does because something about her deserves it. Why doesn't she realize that something is wrong and fix it? Why does she continue in such an uncomfortable state? For a couple of reasons.

First, she probably developed her malfunctioning system in the family where she grew up. Systems like this are often found in families where you're not allowed to be who you are, or have to be something you're not, or in some way are required to redesign yourself. These families often send the message that you can keep the negative to yourself, and the positive isn't meant for you—except as they stipulate, and by then it doesn't even feel positive. So the person develops a system that lets her live in her family, and when she leaves she takes that system with her. She takes it to school and to friendships and to work. All over. And she thinks it's working.

The other reason she keeps the system unchanged is that people generally don't like to change. That doesn't mean they don't want to feel better. They often do. They just want to feel better without changing. Change can be scary, and few of us want to do it without some guarantees. What if you change and you don't feel any better? Then you've lost what you had and are left with nothing. Nobody wants that. We usually feel most comfortable with what we know. It may not be terrific, but at least we're familiar with it and there aren't any surprises.

Besides, the way we see ourselves and our relationship with the world is everything; if we were to change that we'd have to start all over. We'd have to rethink everything—maybe we're OK after all. What would that mean? Well, maybe it would mean that we'd wasted a lot of time on thinking otherwise, and few of us are ready to recognize that we've spent a good deal of our lives believing something that isn't true. So we just keep on with things the way they are. It feels safer.

THINKING STYLES THAT CAN KEEP YOU WHERE YOU ARE

We use some ways of thinking to keep us where we are. Perfectionistic thinking is one of the best ones. Simply put, you think you have to be perfect. It's a strange belief since nobody is, but you cling to it anyway. And "pretty good" doesn't count for anything since it isn't perfect. If you get a B or a C it's considered a failure since it's not an A. If you're not the best in something, you feel like the worst. Only perfect can count. But perfect doesn't usually exist. So every day you set out to do something impossible and then are angry with yourself when you don't succeed. It's enough to keep you stuck in negative feelings for a long, long time. Enough to make you think that maybe the problem is that you're too fat. So you'll focus on your body and decide that if you can just make that perfect you'll feel better.

Another great way to keep yourself where you are is "all or nothing" thinking. With this approach you don't get credit for a part of anything. You have to get the whole thing—and instantly. For example, if you decide to play the piano you don't give yourself time to acquire skill and competence through practice. You have to play at a performance level from the start. If you decide you want to make better grades you have to make them today. You don't give yourself time to develop better study habits and learn what is expected by your teachers. You want an A and you want it now.

The problem with this way of thinking is that learning anything is a process that takes time. You begin at a certain point, and when you've mastered what's there you move on to the next point. When you've finished with that part you go on to the next part—and so on. Learning happens in progressive stages, with each stage building on the previous one. For example, when you were very young you had to learn to crawl before you could walk and had to walk before you could run. You could never have gone straight from crawling to running because your body didn't have the development or experience to get you there.

Inherent in the process of learning is a sense of building and acquiring and integrating, and all of those things take time. But that's what "all or nothing" thinkers don't have. They want it all now. They aren't willing to take the slow, steady route. That would take patience and the ability to work without realizing the reward today. Once again, it's an impossible quest that leaves its owner feeling a failure. So maybe she looks to her body for help and decides that she needs to go on a diet. But she'll probably want that to happen immediately too.

Before I leave "all or nothing," I'd like to put in a plug for "middle ground." It's the place in between. It's the place near "pretty good" or "not bad." I know it may not feel as attractive, but I want to point out that it's from practice and simple piano tunes that one moves toward performance level. It's from the acquisition of better study habits and a sense of what's expected that one is able to improve grades. It's not all, but it's not nothing either, and that doesn't feel half bad sometimes.

Another form of stay-where-you-are behavior is "pedestal thinking." You decide that everybody can do anything better than you can. You put everyone up on a pedestal and then forget that it's you who put them there. You behave as though that's where they naturally belong. But you can't help noticing that everyone is up there but you, so you decide that there must be something right with everybody else and something wrong with you.

This type of thinking is fueled by the tendency to magnify others' strengths and minimize their weaknesses, and, of course, to do just the opposite with yourself. That way you can never bring others down to a more realistic level nor bring yourself up to one. It is guaranteed to keep you where you are.

Another approach is a little different from the ones we've discussed but every bit as powerful in keeping you stuck. It's called catastrophizing, or "the sky is falling" approach. Everything seems to have the potential to become a catastrophe. Therefore, it can be risky to do almost anything, since to do it wrong or make a mistake would be to bring on some horrible outcome.

Catastrophe thinking works partly because it gives everything the same value. For example, any mistake is allowed to feel as terrible as any other mistake. That means that there is no prioritizing or realistic perspective on things. There is just a terrible fear. You don't even try because you can't risk failure—the sky might fall.

People who catastrophize tend to do nothing. They

stay where they are and don't do anything that they can't be sure will succeed. Well, that rules out just about everything; just about anything has risk, and there are few guarantees of success.

KATE

Kate was nineteen and lived with her mother, stepfather, and brother, Jason, who was twelve. Her parents had divorced when she was ten, and her mother had remarried two years later. Actually, her mother had married her boss at work, and Kate never knew if that had started before the divorce or not.

Her father still lived nearby, and she spent weekends with him occasionally. She didn't get along with him as well since she had graduated from high school. He was disappointed that she hadn't gone on to college and didn't understand why she was throwing her life away working part time at a bookstore and still living with her mother. He thought her mother was far too lenient with her, and he didn't like her stepfather. Kate sometimes felt caught in the middle between her parents and often found herself trying to protect one when she was with the other.

Her senior year had been very difficult for her. While she had done well in her grades—that was something she had always worked hard to do—she didn't feel popular enough. She was vice-president of the senior class, but she didn't think that counted for much—she should have been president. She had been on the Homecoming Court, but she hadn't been Queen and that had been a big disappointment. She felt like a failure and was pervasively unhappy. Kate couldn't seem to get herself moving toward college. She had been late with most of her applications and probably wouldn't have sent them in at all if her teachers hadn't pushed her. They didn't understand her difficulty—they felt she had so much "potential"—and didn't take her reluctance seriously. But Kate had always felt uncomfortable when people talked about her potential. It felt like a demand of some kind. Because she had potential—whatever that was—she had to meet these enormously high expectations people had of her. There could be no excuses. She hated it, and she didn't feel ready for whatever the next demand was going to be. She felt scared. And this fear—combined with the guilt she felt about having it—colored most of her senior year.

She was accepted at several of the better schools, and her father was very proud. He even boasted to his friends about his daughter's accomplishment. But he was angry when she didn't follow through and choose one of the schools. He couldn't imagine not wanting to go to an Ivy League school and take advantage of such an opportunity. But she couldn't imagine going.

Her mother was more understanding, saying that if Kate wasn't ready, she could take a year off and live at home while she decided what she wanted to do. But the truth was that her mother and stepfather were fighting a lot these days, and Kate didn't like being around it. Also her mother seemed tired and depressed—especially when her stepfather drank too much.

Kate began to worry more and more about how she looked. She had always been very critical about her body, but now she was even more so. She tried to exercise more and diet off a few pounds, but that didn't seem to help much. She still felt ugly and unattractive.

She looked at the other girls in her class and wondered how they managed to hold everything together so well. They seemed so carefree and happy. They were pretty and popular and didn't even seem to work at it. None of them had any qualms about going away to school. They couldn't wait to get out of the house. Clearly something was wrong with her, but she didn't know how to make it better.

Exercises

What does your interpersonal flow system look like? Try to diagram it with arrows to show what's allowed in and what's allowed out. How does this system let you feel about yourself and others? How flexible is it? Is there much opportunity for mutual impact? What would you change about it if you could? What would you leave the same? Why? What would these changes mean for you?

Do you ever use perfectionistic thinking? Think carefully. What does it tend to do to you? Do you like the way it makes you feel? Do you want to change this? Why?

How much time do you spend in "middle ground"? How much time do you spend in "all or nothing"? What would happen if you were to change this? Could you accept yourself if you weren't as marvelous as you would like to be but not as terrible as you believe yourself to be?

Whom do you put on a pedestal? Why? What does it do to your relationship with that person? What does it make him or her be? What does it make you be? Do you want to change any of this? Why?

How often do you use catastrophe thinking? What effect does it have on you? What does that do for you? What if you were to give it up (even a little bit)? In what direction do you want to go on this? Why?

CHAPTER 10

What Are the Real Chances for Change?

We've talked about many of the pressures that push us to focus on and worry about our bodies. We've looked at the cultural influences that lead us to be dissatisfied with anything short of model-like figures, the pressures that certain kinds of families put on us, the role that unacknowledged feelings play, and the kinds of thinking that keep us stuck in the middle of body distortion and preoccupation.

Given the pressures to stay the same, what are the realistic possibilities for change? I use the word "realistic" purposefully, because that's what anybody who's interested in change wants to know about. Not the pie-in-the-sky chances but the real-in-this-world possibilities. How likely is it that we can change, and how does it happen?

Change that brings new growth and development is difficult, and that's true even if it's change we think we want. Generally when change happens, and it's real, it happens slowly. Sometimes it resembles the way waves wash up on the beach. We reach for a certain change, we make it, and then we settle back to a smaller one. Sometimes it's like the trees in the spring. The greening starts long before it shows, and when it does show, it comes in stages. Real change takes time and goes slowly. We need time to see how it feels and fits us. We need time to make adjustments, make it bigger here and smaller there. We need time to discover what the change will mean for us in ways that we hadn't expected, and to give ourselves a chance to see what we think about it and whether we like it.

That means that if you want to be different you won't be there tomorrow. You'll be starting to think about it and explore it, but you won't be there. It's hard for some of us to have to wait while we slowly develop in a new direction, or wade through a new behavior when it isn't all ours yet. But if change is going to be something we keep and don't throw out the first time it feels funny, it has to work like any other process. Change starts out small and new and gradually becomes bigger and more familiar. It begins unsure and uncomfortable and becomes more confident. At any moment along the way, there is the possibility of throwing it all away and going back to what we used to do, back to where it's familiar. That's the tension of change—the pull between the new and the old, between what we know and what we think we want.

So that is the "realistic" news—you can't have it all now. You can give up and return to the old way of doing things, or you can let yourself try to build a new behavior. But to expect it to be quick and easy is to set yourself up for disappointment, and you already know enough about that.

Another question asked by any serious change-maker is how much can a person really change? That's a question that people in my line of work grapple with all the time, and I don't think we have a really good answer. It probably depends on a number of things, including how much you want the change, how much support you have for obtaining it, how well you're able to continue aiming for it in the face of frustration, and how kind life is to you along the way.

What that boils down to is don't expect too much at first. Plan to change a little. Try to be realistic in your goals, and their attainment becomes that much more likely. If you see that you've achieved a goal, stop and enjoy that victory. Give yourself time to solidify your gains before you press on to the next hurdle. Give yourself a chance to feel the accomplishment your hard work has earned. The way you treat yourself when you reach a goal influences the likelihood of reaching the next one. So when you give yourself a pat on the back, you increase the possibility of further change.

Finally, adolescence is a time of rapid and abundant change. Think of all the changes that are going on in your life at any given moment. Your body is changing—both inside and out, your view of yourself and the world is in flux, your relationship with your parents is changing and can be particularly stormy at times, your relationships with peers are always undergoing ups and downs, your sexuality is emerging in a new way, and you're having to make decisions about behaviors that can have long-term effects. No wonder teenagers feel overwhelmed sometimes.

This makes the kinds of changing we're talking about both easier and harder. Easier because you're still forming and becoming, so things are not quite as solidified as they will be when you're older. Harder because you're already having to respond to so much that it's difficult to take on even a little more. Try not to push yourself to somewhere you aren't able to go. Try to let yourself walk a path that allows you to take advantage of your changeableness yet doesn't add too much additional pressure.

And remember—this is important—you've got a whole lifetime to work on the things we've been talking about. These are not things that anybody solves or is able to fix in a single sitting. All of us have to deal with them, at some level, all the time. We make the best decisions about them that we can at a given moment and then perhaps reevaluate them later when life feels easier or we feel readier, or when circumstances are different and will permit a different outcome.

So the issues I've raised in this book are something for you to begin to think about, consider how important they arc for you, and decide what you might begin to do about them in a way that fits what you're able and willing to manage.

Exercises for Change

I f you decide that you'd like to change some of the ways you think about things and see yourself, there are ways to begin that process. What follows are some exercises that may help to facilitate the change you want.

Try to bring an open mind and a generous heart to the exercises. With one perspective, they can appear trite and silly. With another, they can be an opportunity to see something new or discover another way to feel about yourself. The difference depends on how you approach them and how you approach yourself.

Don't be afraid to do an exercise more than once. Sometimes people find that they have a very different experience each time they try the same thing. Feel free to come back to an exercise when some time has passed, and don't be surprised to discover something new.

Finally, some of you may enjoy doing some of these exercises, as well as those at the end of the chapters, in groups or with friends. It may be fun to discover how differently you see things or to use one another for practice on some of the exercises. I've designated some of them as appropriate for a group setting, but feel free to mix them up anyway you like. Add to them or take away in whatever way makes them best for you.

WRITE A FAIRY TALE
WITH YOU AS HEROINE

Very often we see ourselves as victim, unimportant or powerless. Think of a story in fairy tale language in which you are the one who saves the day. Or is able to change things that need changing. Or rights the wrongs. It really doesn't matter what the story line is or how you write it. But do write it. The written word is more permanent and harder to discount.

This may be hard for some of you. It may feel silly, and it is, in a way. Frankly, I think a little silliness is good for us now and then. But it's not just silly, and that's because it calls on you to think about yourself in a totally new way and then develop a real story around this new character. Writing it as a fairy tale is easier for many people because it's so far removed from how we usually think and talk about ourselves.

After you've developed your story and written it down, read it. How does it feel? Do you like the feeling? What do you like about it? Does it make you uncomfortable? Why? Would you be willing to read your story to someone else? Why? Is this what you expected?

TAKE UP MORE ROOM

Many of us have a tendency to minimize ourselves and feel unimportant. If this is something you do, deliberately try to take up more space. You could do this in many ways, but I'm suggesting that you do it physically. When you walk, take bigger steps. Hold your shoulders back and walk with a longer stride. When you sit down, sprawl out more and take up more room on the chair or couch. At every opportunity try to pull in less and push out more.

It may feel funny at first, and perhaps a little awkward. If that's the case, do it just a little bit and notice how much a little bit feels like a whole lot to you. Then, gradually, try to do more and more. What are your feelings as you move out rather than in? What are you afraid of? What do you hope for? What does it make you want to do? Would that be good for you? Why?

DELIBERATELY MAKE A MISTAKE

So many of us are terrified of mistakes. We have to be perfect and flawless, and we've already talked about what that can do to a person. So let's turn it around. Let's not be afraid of a mistake. Instead, let's choose to make one. Any one. You choose. It might be easier to start with something small and build to something bigger. The important thing is to choose deliberately to do the thing you're so afraid of doing.

What mistake did you choose to make? How did it feel? What did you expect? Were you suprised? Would you be willing to try another one? Do you think this is silly? Do you think trying to be perfect is silly? So what direction do you want to take?

ACCEPT A COMPLIMENT

Many of us are absolutely, positively unable to accept a compliment. Someone says something positive to us and we give it back, pretend they didn't say it, brush it off, move it to the side—in general, do anything we can to behave as though it didn't happen or isn't true. Gracious, how are we ever going to feel better if we don't let in some of the good news?

The next time someone offers you a compliment, STOP. Count to ten and don't say anything. Just see if you can tolerate letting the compliment sit in the air without getting rid of it. If you can do that, see if you can say a simple, "Thank you." You don't have to agree with the person or say you think it's true; just thank the person for the compliment. How do you feel when you don't push it away? What are you afraid of? Does that make sense? Are you allowed to believe good things can be true about you? Would you like to start now?

If you don't feel comfortable waiting for a compliment to float your way naturally, you can always ask someone to help you practice. Ask him or her to say something nice about you and see if you can let it be. And see if you can say thank you. It' hard, isn't it? But you can get better at it.

SAY "NO" TWICE TODAY

Many people find it almost impossible to tell others "No." But like other things, this is a skill you can gain with practice. So let's practice.

Some people find it easier to do this sort of thing if they tell friends and family that it is something they're practicing. Somehow it doesn't feel as threatening if we tell others that we don't mean it, it's just an exercise. It doesn't really matter how you set it up to start. Just start. Say "No." Maybe someone will ask you to do something you don't want to do—say "No." Maybe they'll ask to borrow something you don't want to lend—say "No."

It can be to something small or something big. The object is to practice being able to set a limit that you want to set, to be true to your feelings even if they aren't popular with everyone else. To take the power into your own hands and let someone hear a negative response that you need to give, and to be willing to do it more than once so that you can acquire some comfort with this new skill.

When and where did you say "No"? How did you feel? What were you afraid of? Did it happen? What else happened? Did you like it? Are you willing to try again? Why?

MAKE A LIST OF THINGS YOU ENJOY AND DO ONE TODAY

Sit down in a quiet place and imagine all the things that you enjoy and feel good doing. It can be anything at all so long as you like it. Don't race through it; give yourself a little time to think and explore possibilities. When you've finished, take a look at it. Are there any suprises? Anything you didn't expect? Go through each item and try to remember when you last did this particular thing. Get a sense of how long you've let these things go. How does that feel? Choose one of the items and do it today.

Was it hard to please yourself? Did you enjoy it? Did you feel comfortable? What happens when you take this kind of time and effort for yourself? Do you like that? Do you want it to be different? Why?

DRESS FOOLISHLY FOR A DAY

So much of the time we worry about how we look that it can be fun to turn it around, particularly if we try to look perfect, with nothing out of place. Choose a time to purposely and deliberately look foolish. Choose your clothes to be as silly and mismatched as you can. The more ridiculous the better. The more farfetched, the more likely this exercise will help you.

When you have dressed and can't believe you are actually doing this, go somewhere. It can be anywhere you like. But take yourself as you are, out into the world somewhere, and then return. How did you feel? What did you think others thought? What had you expected would happen? Did it? What do you make of that? Did you learn anything with this effort? What? What will you do with this information?

KEEP A JOURNAL

Many times we're so busy we don't take time to keep a record of what happened and how we're feeling about it. A daily journal is a nice way to keep a running record of our thoughts.

Go to the store and buy a book with blank pages. It should be a book whose appearance pleases you. After all, you're going to be using it every day. Keep it where you can get to it easily.

Try to write in your journal about the same time each day. It's easier to develop a new habit when you have some regularity about it. Don't work too hard at what you write. Just try to think of something of interest or importance for each day. If you can't think of anything, make a note of that fact, but also wonder a bit about it. So much happens each day, it's hard to believe that one went by with no significance. As you begin to develop some familiarity with your journal and writing in it, you'll probably notice that you feel more comfortable with the process. You may find yourself beginning to write more about feelings than events. That's fine, because what you're trying to do is build a relationship with yourself. And you're doing it through a book. Gradually, as you write each day and talk about things that matter, you'll begin to get a sense of yourself and how you feel about things. That's very important knowledge that you can use to help yourself make good decisions.

If you find that journal writing never feels quite right to you, don't worry about it. Some people take to it like a duck to water, and some never feel comfortable with it.

MAKE TWO LISTS: YOUR POSITIVE QUALITIES AND YOUR NEGATIVE QUALITIES

We all have strengths and weaknesses. Every one of us. Sometimes we tend to focus on the negatives because they're the ones that need work. That's fine, but sometimes we focus on them to the exclusion of the good things. That's not so good because then we can forget about our strengths and just see our faults. So make two lists. Don't try to cheat and skip over the positive stuff. It's important. It's what will give you the ability to improve the other.

Look at your lists side by side. What do you think? Were you fair when you made the lists? Did you make an honest effort on both? Look at the negative list; how much time do you spend thinking about these things? Look at the positive list; how much time do you spend recognizing these? Do you need to adjust that pattern? Do you want to? Why? What is that likely to mean for you?

MAKE A SIGN TELLING ABOUT YOUR ACCOMPLISHMENTS

Sometimes we can be very quiet about what we've accomplished. Maybe we don't want to seem stuck up or too proud; but we go too far over on the other side and almost keep them a secret—from ourselves and others. So make a sign that spells out the deeds you can be proud of.

How does it feel to look at it? How does it feel to think of yourself as the person who has done these things? Would you be willing to wear this sign somewhere? OK. Would you be willing to post this sign somewhere? Why? What are you afraid of? Is that realistic? Is that what you want for you?

BALANCE—WHAT'S THAT?

Most of us believe that a well-balanced life is important, but many of us easily forget this notion when we set about living our life. Let's see how your balance feels.

Generally speaking, a good life needs work and play, and discipline and generosity, and exercise and relaxation, and satisfaction and challenge, and togetherness and aloneness, and so on. Make your own list of the kinds of things that a well-balanced life needs.

Now, consider your own life and see what's there and what's missing of the things you think are important. Make a list of what's in your life. Make a second list of what's not there. What are your thoughts as you look at the two lists? What kind of person do you think the first list would make? What about the second list? What would a person be like if her life included things on both lists? Would you like to be like that? Why?

Decide what you think would be the most important thing to add to your life. How would you do it? Would you need to go slowly, or could you do something more quickly? Add something to your life in the way that feels most comfortable to you.

Was this easy or difficult? Try it again. Was that easier? A lot of times things are hardest when they are brand-new, so don't give up. Sometimes things are hard if we don't think we deserve them. Is that getting in your way? Try not to let it. That's "stay where you are and don't change" thinking. If you're serious about change you need to give yourself a chance.

CURIOUS INSTEAD OF CRITICAL

To many of us nothing comes easier than being critical with ourselves. Considering how damaging that can be, it's amazing how easily it comes. You look at yourself and you see the flaws; you look at something you've done and you see what you didn't do, and so on.

Let's try a new perspective. Let's be curious, not critical, about ourselves. See if you can pretend that you're meeting yourself for the first time and you want to know what you're like. This means that you haven't had a chance to develop all the notions about yourself that you've saved and compiled throughout the years. You don't already know all your flaws and weak points that you tend to zero in on when thinking about yourself.

This is a totally different process. It is completely nonjudgmental. There is no value system. Nothing is considered better or worse. There is only, "What am I like?" Without the usual fear of failing, it may be easier for you to take an honest look and discover some things that may surprise you, or, if not suprise, feel different in this new context of "no criticism." This curious not critical stance is one of the most difficult things for a person to master. Don't expect it to work all at once. It will take time, and you will need to learn to trust yourself not to jump back into that critical mode. But if you can begin to change your perspective even the least bit, it will make a difference. It is an accepting perspective that lets us grow, and it is a curious look that lets us discover who we are.

INVITE A DRAGON TO TEA

All of us have things that we really fear. Sometimes they're things that make sense (war, for example), but sometimes they're things that we don't need to be so frightened of (such as failure). We tend to give these fears a great deal of power and let them become bigger than they should be. Then we behave as if they're really as big and powerful and terrible as we've made them, and we let them make us afraid to encounter them. So we don't. We manage to avoid them. We think the reason we're safe is because we've avoided the dragons, and we never have an opportunity to learn differently.

By never encountering what scares us, we never have

a chance to discover that these things are not as unbear-
able or frightening as we've imagined. We never have a
chance to learn that we're strong enough to endure
them. We don't have a chance to develop the skills to do
battle with them when we need to, and that makes us
less than we can be.

So how about meeting your fears? Or fighting your
dragons? Or, as I like to think about it, having your
dragon to tea. I think what I like about this image is that
it's a small step. You don't have to go out and do full
battle, but you have a chance to meet your fear and get
to know it better. You get to learn where it comes from
and what supports it and how it gets stronger and what
you can do to make it smaller. It's a friendly gesture
toward something that you don't typically feel friendly with, and that can begin to change the nature of your
relationship with your fear and yourself. When you
aren't as scared of something, you can look at it differently, and when you can see something in better
perspective, you can discover other ways to feel about it.
When you're not so frightened of something, you have
more room to move around in the world; you don't have
to hold yourself so tightly, and it feels better.

So choose a fear that you would like to work on. It's
probably a good idea to choose one that feels possible for
this exercise—not the biggest one you've got!

Imagine what this fear looks like. That sounds a little
silly, but if you can imagine something you can begin to
understand it. Imagine this fear in any way that makes
sense to you, and don't worry about its being a little
silly. Once you've imagined it, you can invite it to visit
you. Maybe not for tea—but maybe to come close
enough for you to see it and begin to get a feel for it.

Maybe you can begin to get a sense of what it is about you that has let this fear grow so large or feel so scary or threatening. You don't have to figure out the whole thing the first time you try this. Aim for a small understanding; then you can build on this experience the second time. The important thing to remember is that you are the one who is giving this fear so much power. Wouldn't it be nice to know why?

BODY COLORING

For this exercise, you'll need a sheet of paper and some crayons, colored pencils, or Magic Markers. Draw the outline of a female body. It doesn't have to be perfect—not even very good. Just something to serve as a way to think about your whole body. Now choose five colors to stand for the different ways you might feel about different parts of your body. Let one color stand for very positive, one for moderately positive, one for neutral, one for moderately negative, and one for very negative. Now color the body according to the way you see your own. For example, if you feel very positive about your feet, color them accordingly. If you feel neutral about your hair, color it that way. You may find that you color most of the body one color, or you may have lots of colors for different parts. It doesn't matter. Just do it according to how you feel about yourself.

When you've finished, stop and think about what you just did. How did it feel to consider all of your body and judge your feelings about it? Did you have to think about it? Did anything surprise you? Look at the parts you feel best about. How do you treat them? Look at the parts you feel worst about. How do you treat them? If there are parts that you feel very negative about, consider what it is like to go into the world feeling that way about a part of yourself. What does it do to you? How does it make you feel with others? Is this the way you want to treat yourself? Why? Would it be possible for you to be kinder to your body and more forgiving? Why? What does this mean for you?

GROUP EXERCISES

Blow Up a Balloon

Sit in a circle and pass around a bag of balloons. Ask each person to choose a balloon and give the single instruction, "Put enough air in it." Give everyone time to blow up the balloons and tie them off. Then go around the circle and let each person talk about how she approached the question, "How much is enough?"

Most of us have trouble knowing when we've done enough, had enough, are full enough, have eaten enough, are thin enough, are smart enough, are pretty enough, and so on. This exercise is a very simple and concrete way for each person to address the question for herself and create her own balloon. Sometimes a person thinks enough is blowing the balloon to the point of almost popping. That will leave her with a very strained and fragile balloon. Sometimes a person doesn't know how much is enough until she's looked around the room to see what everybody else is doing. That makes it hard to get going on your balloon! Sometimes a person just doesn't feel she has the energy to blow the balloon up. That can leave her out of the game and feeling a failure.

Give each person a chance to talk about her experience. And remember—there's no right answer, there's no right amount, and there's no balloon that's better than another. It's all a way of learning how you approach things. It all depends on what you want your balloon to do.

Come as Yourself Ten Years From Now

Invite your friends to come to a group as themselves ten years from now. This is a little like dress-ups and a little like theater. Each person is asked to dress, look, and act as herself in the future.

When your guests arrive, treat it as a reunion. Gather in a circle, and give each person a chance to talk about herself. It's often particularly useful to ask about the best and hardest parts of her life now, the hardest part of the past ten years and how she coped with it, the biggest surprise of the past ten years, and the thing that has surprised her least. Any question that encourages her to think about herself from a perspective other than the one she has in the present is particularly helpful. When a person has finished talking about herself and answering questions, ask how it felt to talk about herself as she just did. Sometimes people feel that the pretend was really possible, and sometimes they think it was not. It's important to know where we think we can go and where we think we're not allowed.

The goal of this exercise is to encourage someone to "try something on," to see how it feels and reject or accept it as a possibility. We often don't give ourselves much of an opportunity to try; we think we have to succeed. This is a chance to explore safely without the necessity of doing it. Since I think we often go toward where we believe we are moving, it's good to have a sense of where you are trying to go.

Body Painting

Most of us look at our bodies as something that has to be beautiful and perfect. This is an attempt to see your body in another way—as a canvas.

This exercise works best if you have a good-size mirror available in which everyone can see themselves as they work. Washable crayons or paints work best. Wear clothing you don't care about so that if you get something on it (even though it will probably wash out) you won't have to worry.

The goal of this exercise is to decorate or color as much or as little of your body as you can. If you can, start with your face. Some people find this too uncomfortable; if you do, find the part that you can manage. You can try to do something specific, like making a mask with color, or you can follow the contours of your body and make a design according to the pattern your body creates, or you can simply put on color or designs randomly. There's no one way or right way to do this. There's simply seeing what you can try and how it turns out and how that makes you feel.

Try to resist the temptation to make yourself pretty. We do that all the time. Try to make this time different. Sometimes people discover things they hadn't expected, such as that making a mask on their face feels safer, or feels scary, or fun. Sometimes they discover that the only part of their body they can color is their hands. That's important to know if part of changing is knowing where you're allowed to explore and where you're not.

Try not to make this anything but a chance to discover, and see what you learn.

Tell a Group Story

This tends to work best with at least four storytellers, but do it with as many as you have. Sit in a circle and tell a sequential story: One person starts a story and tells as much of it as she wants, then hands it to the next girl, who picks it up, continues or changes it in any way she wishes, and then hands it on. It can go on forever, but usually the group decides at some point that this is the final round.

When the story is over, discuss how each of you felt while telling your part and watching what happened to it as it left you and went round the room. Was there somebody in the group who always saved the hero or heroine just as she was about to meet his or her doom? Did your story have a hero or heroine, and what does that mean? Was somebody always trying to make the story sad or scary? Was there someone who always tried to make it safe? Notice what part each of you played, and see what that tells you about yourself.

Do a Body Tracing

Sometimes it's very hard to see our body as it is. We look at ourselves in the mirror and start getting critical before we can really see what's there. This is a chance to change the format of a self-look.

You'll need some large pieces of paper and brief or tight-fitting clothing. Tape sheets together so that you can lie down with your legs and arms extended. Take turns being drawn and doing the drawing. Use a Magic Marker to outline the body, slanting the pen toward the body a bit so that it stays close to the shape you're trying to copy.

After everyone has had a tracing done, give each person a chance to look at her drawing and talk about her reactions to it. Let others give feedback on whether they think it looks accurate. Sometimes people know so little about how they look that they can't tell when a drawing resembles their shape. The group's feedback can be an important teaching tool.

Sometimes the drawing looks worse than the person thought it would; sometimes it looks better. Sometimes she doesn't know how she feels. But it's a chance to learn all of that and, perhaps, understand better how she feels about her body's shape.

Make a List of "Must Be's" and "Must Not Be's" for an American Female

Put some large sheets of paper on the wall. Get everyone together and brainstorm about all the things that you are supposed to be—physically, emotionally, spiritually, personally, academically, athletically, and so on. Make a list as long as the things your group can think of.

Now make the opposite list, all the things that you're not allowed to be as a female in America. Keep going for as long as you can.

When you've finished both lists, look at them. First, the "Must Be" list. Does anyone in your group know anyone who is all those things? Does anyone think it is even possible to be all those things? What do you think it would do to a person to believe she had to be all those things?

Look at the "Must Not" list. Does anyone know anybody who isn't any of those things? Do you think it is possible to not be any of those things? What do you think it would do to a person to believe she couldn't be any of those things? Now see if your group can create a third list: a list of what women should realistically set as goals to aim for.

Appendix A

Some Facts about Bodies and Eating Disorders

1. Ninety percent of bulimics and 90 to 95 percent of anorectics are female.
2. Anorexia's mortality rate is about 10 percent (it kills one out of ten people who have it), and that's the highest of any psychiatric illness.
3. Women have a lower resting metabolic rate than men and require fewer calories for life-sustaining functions.
4. Records of body measurements indicate that Miss America contestants, *Playboy* centerfolds, Barbie Dolls, and female models have become increasingly thin over time.
5. The act of dieting can result in a reduced metabolic rate, thereby making weight loss more difficult (and frustration that much greater).
6. Several studies indicate that females tend to overestimate their body size (while men are significantly more accurate), thereby increasing their tendency to feel fat and need to diet. In one study those women happiest with their weight were about ten pounds below average for their height.
7. After puberty, girls naturally have almost twice as much body fat as boys.
8. The incidence of eating disorders among women on college campuses has been estimated to be as high as 20 percent.
9. Some studies suggest that restrictive dieting is the most frequently reported precipitating event leading to the development of bulimia.

10. A study of thirteen-year-olds indicated that 80 percent of the girls had been on a weight-loss diet and only 10 percent of the boys.
11. Anorexia can result in gastrointestinal problems, depression, headaches, low pulse and temperature, sensitivity to cold, weakness, low blood sugar, fainting, and hair loss.
12. Bulimia can result in heart failure, tooth loss, gum disease, electrolyte imbalance, headaches, depression, gastrointestinal problems, skin irritations, and large weight fluctuations.
13. Weight watching and dieting are so pervasive among girls and women that they have become the norm.

Appendix B

Resources

If you are having trouble with anorectic or bulimic behavior, several national self-help organizations have local groups across the country. They should be able to refer you to someone in your area who can help you find a therapist or connect you with people who are struggling with the same issues you are. Here are the addresses and phone numbers of the organizations' headquarters.

American Anorexia/Bulimia Association, Inc. (AABA)
133 Cedar Lane
Teaneck, NJ 07666
(201) 836–1800
(AABA publishes a newsletter)

Anorexia Nervosa and Related Eating Disorders, Inc. (ANRED)
P.O. Box 5102
Eugene, OR 97405
(503) 344–1144

Bulimia/Anorexia Self-Help (BASH)
Deaconess Hospital
6150 Oakland Avenue
St. Louis, MO 63139
(314) 991–BASH or (800) BAS-HSTL
(BASH publishes a newsletter)

National Association of Anorexia Nervosa and Associated Disorders (ANAD)
P.O. Box 271
Highland Park, IL 60035
(312) 831–3438

Suggested Reading

Bruch, Hilde. *Eating Disorders: Obesity, Anorexia Nervosa and the Person Within.* New York: Basic Books, 1973.

This is a well-written book that gives a broad view of the etiology of obesity and anorexia. Its author was a pioneer in the treatment of eating disorders. Even if some of the text is too heavy for you, the case studies are interesting.

————. *The Golden Cage.* New York: Vintage Books, 1979.

This book by Ms. Bruch is more readable than her first one. It gives a very clear picture of the types of families that contribute to development of anorexia and the girls who try to express themselves through the disorder.

Chernin, Kim. *The Hungry Self.* New York: Times Books, 1985.

Written by a woman who struggled with an eating disorder for years and now treats others with the problem, this book explores the troubled relationship between a mother and daughter as the root of an eating disorder. Ms. Chernin pursues the same themes in a number of other books, including *The Obsession* and *In My Mother's House.*

Lawrence, Marilyn (ed). *Fed Up and Hungry.* New York: Peter Bedrick Books, 1987.

A collection of essays about eating disorders with a feminist perspective.

Levenkron, Steven. *Best Little Girl in the World.* New York: Warner Books, 1979.

The author has worked with eating disorders for some time, and this tells the story of a composite of his patients. A very readable book. He follows a similar vein with *Kessa*.

O'Neill, Cherry Boone. *Starving for Attention.* New York: Continuum, 1983.

The daughter of singer and actor Pat Boone, Ms. O'Neill tells the story of her many years with an eating disorder and her road to recovery.

Orbach, Susie. *Hunger Strike. The Anorectic's Struggle as Metaphor for Our Age.* New York: W.W. Norton & Co., 1986.

An interesting view of anorexia—as both an expression of our cultural mandate and an act of rebellion against it. Ms. Orbach lives in England and does most of her work with eating disorder patients there.

———. *Fat Is a Feminist Issue.* New York: The Berkley Publishing Group, 1978.

A self-help book for compulsive overeaters, with a section on anorexia. Some interesting ideas about what getting fat and trying to be thin are really about (not what you think!)

I believe that eating disorders and problems with body-image are, in fact, problems of growing up. We all have problems growing, but some of us get stuck deeper in the mud than others. One of the ways to begin to get unstuck is to better understand yourself and the people around you, and one of the nicest ways to do that is through good books. So I have included the following as a possible starting point.

Auel, Jean M. *The Clan of the Cave Bear*. New York: Crown Publishers, 1980.

This is the story of Ayla, a beautiful girl who lived during prehistoric times. An orphan as a small child, she was adopted by another tribe but was ridiculed and rejected because she didn't have the flat head tribe members had and refused to accept their rules about female behavior. A nicely told story that combines current themes with an ancient setting.

Austen, Jane. *Pride and Prejudice*. New York: Washington Square Press, 1982.

I recommend just about any Jane Austen book; she is a wonderful observer of human kind. This one and *Sense and Sensibility* are particularly good. They paint pictures of families and relationships that are as apt today as when she wrote them in the 1800's.

Burnett, Frances Hodgson. *The Secret Garden*. New Jersey: Dell Publishing Co., 1938.

This is a wonderful story about several children from very different backgrounds and how they influence and change each other and discover the best parts of themselves.

de Saint Exupery, Antoine. *The Little Prince*. New York: Harcourt, Brace, Jovanovich, 1943.

This is a story about a little Prince who lives alone on a tiny planet no bigger than a house. It details his travels to other planets and the things he learns from the people and animals that he meets. The young prince discovers wisdom that some adults never find.

Guest, Judith. *Ordinary People*. New York: Random House, 1976.

A powerful story about a family that loses its oldest son in a boating accident, it shows us how the three remaining family members deal with the loss and, in particular, how the surviving brother manages his feelings.

Juster, Norton. *The Phantom Toll Booth*. New York: Random House; 1961.

This is a wonderful book about a boy's travels through the Kingdom of Wisdom and his attempt to rescue the Princesses Rhyme and Reason and bring them back to their throne. As you can see, there's lovely playing on words that makes the book both wise and very funny.

Lobel, Arnold, *Frog and Toad Together*. New York: Harper & Row, 1971.

This book is intended for young readers, but it has a lot to say to all of us—especially the story entitled, "The Garden." A very amusing yet clear tale about our impatience with the time it takes things to grow and develop.

———. *Owl at Home*. New York: Harper & Row, 1975.

Another book for younger readers, but you shouldn't miss the story entitled, "Upstairs and Downstairs." It captures the difficulty of trying to do the impossible.

Silverstein, Shel. *The Missing Piece*. New York: Harper & Row, 1976.

Silverstein writes wonderfully, and in this book he does it with lots of good pictures and a minimum of text. This is a must read for anyone who is looking for someone else to make her complete. I also recommend *Looking for the Big O*. They're in the youth section of the library, but they speak to us all.

Wharton, William. *Dad*. New York: Knopf, 1981.

This book tells about the dance that families do as well as any I know. It gives us a simultaneous glimpse of a man as both son and father. Very touching and beautifully written. Wharton also wrote *Birdy*, which is good, but I like this best.

Williams, Margery. *The Velveteen Rabbit.* New York: Doubleday & Co., Inc., 1922.

A classic story about a rabbit's journey from being a plush and shiny velveteen toy to a wiser and more tattered real rabbit. Has some classic passages about the difficult process of maturing and how most of us would rather avoid the discomfort that is part of the journey.

Index